One Thread in God's Rich Tapestry

The Story of Ian Longfield

Jim Cockburn

GRACE
PUBLISHING
Dyslexic Friendly

First published 2020 by Malcolm Down Publishing Ltd
www.malcolmdown.co.uk

24 23 22 21 20   7 6 5 4 3 2 1

British Library Cataloguing in Publication Data
A catalogue record for this book is available from the British Library.

ISBN 978-1-912863-55-6

Cover design by Esther Kotecha
Art direction by Sarah Grace

Printed in the UK

Contents

Preface

Ian Longfield is a remarkable Christian man who has had a wonderful impact on the lives of so many people in the community in which he lived and worked, the post-war Longbenton council estate on the outskirts of Newcastle upon Tyne. He also had a major influence on the wider spiritual life of Tyneside.

As the local general practitioner, he cared deeply for the medical needs of the families who lived on the estate and who came to his practice, and he and his wife Helen worked hard to meet these needs. He also cared deeply for their spiritual needs, praying that many would come to a living faith in the Lord Jesus Christ; prayers were answered through the establishment of Somervyl Chapel on the estate and the blessings that flowed from it.

I first met Ian not long after I took up my position in 1993 as principal of Longbenton Community College, the comprehensive school that served the catchment area of Somervyl Chapel and Ian's practice. Ian and his wife Helen were key members of a prayer meeting that met in my office to pray for the needs of the school, praying that God would protect and sustain the students and staff and that we would have opportunities to point people to Jesus. I realised from my early encounters with Ian that he was a man of great wisdom and biblical insight, with a heart that was very much for the Lord and the people of Longbenton. I was humbled that he, Helen and other Christians would commit themselves to praying regularly for my school and myself. His prayers and words of encouragement did much to strengthen me in my role.

As I have undertaken research for this book, I have come to realise in a new light the impact of the legacy of Ian Longfield and Somervyl Chapel on Longbenton. I recall my chair of governors talking about the riots that took place in the Meadow Well district of North Shields in 1991, and saying that they could so easily have taken place in Longbenton as it had a similar demographic to Meadow Well. He felt that the riots had not spread to Longbenton because of the influence of the school of which I was now principal. That is only partly true; what was more significant was that Ian and the members of Somervyl Chapel had a profound spiritual influence on the estate over three decades, covering the estate with deep prayer, seeking the Lord's blessing and protection for the estate.

His influence did, however, spread much wider than Longbenton, as he prayed continually for spiritual revival across the region. He longed to see people across Tyneside commit themselves to Christ and be changed by the working of his Holy Spirit. He also longed to see Bible-believing church leaders united in their vision for the Lord. In furthering this vision he worked very closely with church leaders in the region from a variety of denominations, some of whom would call themselves charismatic and some of whom would come from a more reformed tradition. He seemed to be able to win the confidence of Christians from a variety of denominations and persuasions, and, for example, used his influence to start regular meetings for Christian leaders across Tyneside held in the Mansion House in Newcastle.

Ian Longfield has, through the grace of God, touched the lives of countless people over his long life and ministry. The people that he worked alongside or to whom he ministered and gave medical and spiritual care are very much aware that there was something very special about Ian. His wife Helen is also held in very high regard for her never-failing support for Ian and her own spiritual wisdom and kindness.

His close friend Robert Ward, vicar of St Luke's Church in Spital Tongues, Newcastle described him as *"very loving with a heart for poor people, a brave, pioneering man, an encourager, persistent, enabling and supportive"*.

Valerie Wadge, working alongside him in the practice, saw that he was *"extremely caring for the people of Longbenton"*.

Mike Johnson from the Newcastle Reformed Evangelical Church and treasurer of the Tyneside Leadership Forum admired *"his get up and go attitude"*.

Mark Sharman, pastor of Somervyl Chapel in the 1980s, described him as *"a father of the faith"*.

Ken Prudhoe, a former member of Somervyl Chapel and himself a general practitioner, felt that he was *"tireless in his medical work and church responsibilities, remaining cheerful and uncomplaining, never satisfied and always seeking more and better blessings for the church"*. Rosie, Ken's wife, remembered him as someone who was *"a huge influence for good, stable and godly living"* and who displayed *"mutual respect even though Ian was older and wiser"*.

Ian is now in his nineties, and for some time he has felt that the Lord was prompting him to record his life story as an encouragement to Christians to serve God faithfully and effectively wherever he has placed them. About ten years ago, his great friend and prayer partner, Mervyn Spearing, suggested that he should write his story. Ian thought about it over a number of years, until God put it clearly on his heart at a prayer meeting he attended in 2015. This meeting was led by members of the Glasgow Prophetic Centre. Although Ian had a natural caution about prophecies, he felt that those taking the meeting were biblical in their outlook as they spoke about the need for repentance and forgiveness. One of the team, Sarah-Jane Biggart, prophesied over Ian telling him that he should tell his story as he had a lot in his heart and mind, and that he should buy a

Dictaphone and record it. The fact that she spoke of "recording" the story was significant for Ian, as by then his sight had deteriorated so far that there was no way in which he could have "written" it. As Ian commented later, *"That rather shook me and I took it seriously to heart and began to think about my story and particularly about the spiritual pilgrimage that I have had and the things that God has revealed to me over the years."*

The following, then, is Ian Longfield's story, taken largely from his Dictaphone recordings. In a sense, however, it is not about Ian but rather about God who was always in front, leading one of his people into avenues of service to further his Kingdom. Ian had a picture in his mind of God creating a beautiful tapestry; God was the master weaver and Ian was but one thread in God's rich tapestry. May it encourage others to follow God's voice and discern where he wants to use them for his glory as he creates his awesome tapestry.

Acknowledgements

Many people who knew Ian and Helen well provided me with insights into their lives and ministries. I am very grateful to the following who gave up their time to speak to me: Peter Bentley, Reverend George Curry, Doctor Tim Dunnett, Dave Glover, Sue Glover, Maurice Gunn-Russell, Doctor Neil Gunn-Russell, Reverend David Holloway, Mike Johnson, John McKale, Doctor Ken Prudhoe, Doctor Rosie Prudhoe, Mark Sharman, Right Reverend David Smith, Eddie Stringer, Doctor Valerie Wadge, Reverend Doctor Robert Ward and Simon Warren.

I am particularly grateful for the patience of Ian and Helen themselves, along with their son David, as I continually went back to them to seek further clarification. The last chapter in the book in particular is very much the product of David's thinking as he looked back over how the Lord worked in his father's life, in the service of God and others. I hope that this small volume accurately reflects the story they wanted told.

Grateful thanks are also due to Jane van Es and Barrie Craven who generously gave up their time to proofread the text. Jim Swan has freely given us the use of photographs that he had previously taken of Ian and Helen.

Malcolm Down of Malcolm Down and Sarah Grace Publishing provided invaluable support and advice.

Jim Cockburn
2020

Chapter One
Early Years

Ian was born in 1927 in Newcastle into what he describes as a very privileged family. He was an only child and enjoyed a very advantaged, protected childhood. His grandfathers were successful in business, one in the fruit trade into which Ian's own father entered in due course, and the other as an agent for an Edinburgh brewer. Although Ian did not go into business himself he inherited an entrepreneurial streak from them that would be used by God in his future work as a church leader initiating new activity and taking risks for the Lord.

They were a good family, and in Ian's own words, *"nice people but with not much thought for God"*. Although Ian's background was not really Christian, God had his hand upon him. To quote Ian on his early religious views,

> *I always had a feeling in my spirit that Jesus was important, that his teaching was to be followed and that his lifestyle was brilliant. Right up through my teens I had sought to follow him. In a sense I was a nice guy but "nice" is not a biblical word and doesn't carry any weight with God. But I did try, went to church a bit, and so on.*

As a child he was sent to a private school, the Newcastle Preparatory School, where he was forced to wear a white stiff collar, something that added to his overall dislike of school. He enjoyed the second half of his education much more, because there was a greater emphasis on sports and games, and Ian displayed great prowess on the sports field.

Ian started his secondary education at the beginning of the Second World War. The Leys School, based in Cambridge, had been evacuated to the Pitlochry Atholl Palace Hotel in the Scottish Highlands because Addenbrooke's Hospital was taking over their school buildings for war casualties. The school was relocated to Pitlochry for the duration of the war, and by God's providence in the summer before the school moved, Ian and his parents stayed in the hotel on holiday and met some of the school staff who were getting ready for the great upheaval that was to take place. Ian's father was impressed by the staff and so enrolled Ian at the school. This was where Ian was educated for the next five years.

Ian felt that although he was not academically brilliant, he got on well, becoming head boy and captain of both the rugby and cricket teams. He was certainly held in high regard at the school, as indicated by a thank-you letter from his housemaster, Mr Mellor, sent in 1946. It starts off very formally, *"Dear Longfield"*, but concludes very warmly by saying, *"No boy, in my memory, has ever done more, and it was a great help to me to know that I had the backing of yourself and your splendid body of prefects. When all the world is so unsettled, I place it largely to your credit that the tone of the school is at present so high."*

Despite his alleged lack of academic calibre, he won a place at Clare College, Cambridge to read history, although his wife Helen later joked that this might have been more to do with his sporting ability, which in those days counted much more in gaining entry to the top institutions of learning in the country.

In 1946 he left school, but before he could take up his Cambridge place, he had to undergo his national service, which was still operating even though the war had ended. He was called up into the army, where he served for just under two years, starting in Richmond in

Yorkshire with six weeks of square bashing getting sore feet from the boots, before moving on to officer training at Aldershot. Ultimately he got a commission and became a second lieutenant. He was sent up to Perth in Scotland, where he was stationed for nearly a year.

Something very strange happened on New Year's Eve 1947, which Ian remembers very clearly as one of the most significant events in his life.

I had been home for the Christmas holidays and was returning in the dark by myself in an old-fashioned compartment on the train from Edinburgh to Perth. I was sitting alone in the compartment thinking about the New Year and how going to study history at Cambridge seemed rather pointless and without a future. This made me decide that I had better pray. I had never done anything like this in regard to a big decision before, but in that cold dark compartment I prayed, "What should I do?" Then like a bolt in my head, coming in the right-hand side, in the right temple, and going through my head came very clearly, "Be a doctor." It was quite extraordinary, very meaningful and very clear and I never for a moment doubted it again. Twenty minutes later I got off the train, walked back to my billet, knowing that I was going to be a doctor.

God spoke to Ian in a clear, amazing way, even though he was not yet a Christian. God had wonderful plans for Ian's life!

Ian told his parents who were very supportive of his decision. He contacted the college, and the Master agreed to take him in as a medical student rather than a history student. This was amazing, as Ian had not even studied science at A-level. When he went up to Cambridge, he joined a small group of about ten students who, like him, had not studied sciences but were starting the medical course.

They had to start at the beginning studying basic physics, chemistry and biology, which was extremely hard work, but he persevered and enjoyed it. It was very much learning by "cramming" rather than by understanding, but it paid off, so much so that his tutor perhaps jokingly felt that he should be studying chemistry rather than medicine!

Cambridge

During his first year at Cambridge, Ian was in residence in the college, which was a highly beneficial experience for him as he was able to mix in easily with other students. For the next two years he was out in digs as there was not enough space in college for all students. He was very fortunate to go with an old school friend, Donald McMillan, to stay with a widow called Mrs Pendlebury in Barrow Road in a very pleasant part of Cambridge. She had a very sad story: she and her husband had been archaeologists in Crete and, at the beginning of the Second World War, she remained in England while her husband returned to Crete as a soldier involved in preparing the resistance against the forthcoming German invasion of the island. He was tragically wounded in the Battle of Crete and then later shot as a spy. She looked after Ian and Donald very well during their time living in her house.

Ian had an intellectual belief in Jesus when he went to Cambridge and would go to the local Methodist church occasionally. His friend, Ron Pont, a fellow medical student who was a fine Christian, had a great influence on his life at this time. On a Saturday night as Ian was going off to the local dance, Ron would ride past him on his bicycle and shout, "Hello, Ian, I am off to the Bible study." Ron's influence finally led Ian to surrendering his life to Jesus in the middle of the first term of his third and final year at Cambridge. He had a really wonderful conversion experience, which he described as follows:

Charlie Moule, the dean of our College, was a very well-known gentle, fatherly chaplain and also Professor of New Testament Theology. He had arranged a little mission in the college and for a week Archdeacon Harrison from Sheffield gave evening talks. On the Tuesday evening I was there, and he explained the gospel in a very clear way so that I really understood it. His text was, "For God so loved the world that he gave his only begotten son that whosoever believeth in him should not perish but have everlasting life,"[1] and my eyes were opened. I realised that it wasn't any good just trying to be a Christian, but rather it was having God save me from sin and him coming into my life. This was a very, very wonderful experience. I cycled back to my digs on air and stayed on air for about two or three months. This led me to relate much more with other Christian people for the last few months at Cambridge.

This experience was a very significant turning point in Ian's spiritual life, and would have a profound effect on him throughout his life. Many years later, on his ninetieth birthday, Ian received a card from Clare College with a photograph of the college. Of all the views of the college that could have been sent to Ian, what was amazing was that it showed a view of the chapel door through which he had entered to give his life to the Lord.

Ian enjoyed his time in Cambridge with Donald, who actually became President of the Union, which meant that he had to organise and preside over the greatly renowned Cambridge debating society. Once his academic studies at Cambridge came to an end, he said

---

1   John 3:16 (Authorised Version)

goodbye to Donald as he moved on to the Royal London Hospital to start his three years of medical training.

London

Ian found his medical training hard work but very enjoyable. He had to travel in from digs out in Ilford for the first year and then obtained accommodation in the student residences beside the hospital in Whitechapel. Being nearby enabled him to get much more involved in the life of the hospital. He played rugby for the hospital team in his first year and was appointed vice-captain in his second. In the second match of that season, however, having scored two tries (which was very unusual for a second row forward), he unfortunately wrenched his knee badly. He damaged the cartilage and had to have it operated on, but the operation did not go well; the knee became infected and he was never able to play rugby again, which was a great disappointment.

Ian finished his training, passed his exams and was given two "house jobs" in the hospital. These were very prestigious jobs, one with the Professor of Surgery, Walter Dix, and another with Donald Hunter, a very well-known consultant physician. Ian felt very fortunate, loving what he was doing without being too hard-working. He was on one of two wards that worked together. His colleague on the other ward liked to go out on a Saturday night, and so Ian covered for him then; in return, he covered for Ian on a Sunday morning to enable him to go to church.

When Ian went up to London, he met up with lots of Christians, particularly those from Brethren assemblies. He enjoyed their company and went with them to house parties, Bible studies and Brethren meetings. Very soon, however, he found his way to Westminster Chapel where he thoroughly enjoyed deep and inspiring teaching from Doctor Martyn Lloyd-Jones, as well as occasionally going to hear John Stott at All Souls, Langham Place.

At that time Ian and his friends in digs used to meet in one of their rooms every evening for a quick prayer before going to bed. These were heady and happy days for a young Christian.

Ian was fortunate to be training in London at the time of the 1954 Harringay Crusade, led by the fiery young American evangelist Billy Graham. This was an exciting time for Christians in London, as an estimated two million people went to hear the gospel through Billy Graham's inspired preaching. Ian took the opportunity to invite student friends to the crusade meetings, and they were moved by the sincerity and devotion of the evangelist and by the message he preached.

During his time in London, Ian needed to consider where he would undertake his medical practice. His Brethren friends all went abroad as medical missionaries. The great challenge at that time for any self-respecting young Christian medical student was to go and serve God in the less developed countries of the world. Two friends went as missionaries to northern Nigeria, another went to what was then Northern Rhodesia (now Zambia), while Ron Pont, who had been so influential in Ian becoming a Christian, went a few years later with his wife Molly to Iran and then to Pakistan.

It was only really later that Ian realised why he had not done the same. He had begun to get trouble with his eyesight; he had conical corneas and slowly his vision deteriorated, which meant that he would not be able to perform surgery, something that would be expected of a medical missionary. Within a few years he had to have a corneal graft on one eye. It was extremely successful and enabled him to drive and to practise medicine for thirty years. Later he needed the other eye to be operated on and then a second graft on the first eye. Although these operations enabled him to see throughout his working life, over time his eyesight suffered gradual deterioration and he is now registered as partially blind.

Back to the North-East

After finishing his house jobs in London he decided to come back to Newcastle in 1955. In preparation for general practice, he took a six-month obstetric job at Dilston Hall, a maternity hospital near Hexham. Ian enjoyed being back in the north-east, practising medicine in such a beautiful setting. Following Dilston Hall, he trained as a general practitioner in Earsdon and its surrounding villages, close to the seaside resort of Whitley Bay.

Ian had enjoyed wonderful Christian fellowship in London and so now that he was back in the north-east, it was vital that he found a church where he could continue to grow as a Christian and serve and worship the Lord. He enquired at the Bible House, a Christian bookshop formerly in the centre of Newcastle, regarding possible evangelical churches. He was recommended to go to the Central Hall in the Elswick district of Newcastle. He took this advice, became a member of this fellowship, and then shortly afterwards he was invited to join their "executive" team. It was an outgoing, Bible-teaching church, with an emphasis on youth work. This was to be his church until he and his family later left for Longbenton with their blessing.

One of his gifts that would be developed in the coming years would be preaching. Although he had done a little bit of preaching in London, it was his first sermon in the north-east that had particular significance, and as he recalled: *"At some point, rather amusingly, a local Methodist minister who had taken an interest in me when I first arrived home sent me down to preach my first sermon, and can you believe it? It was in a little wooden community hut in the newly built Longbenton estate, which was later to become my mission field! This set me on a path to do a lot of local preaching in Methodist, Brethren and other chapels and missions for many years."* On that occasion he preached on John 3:16, the verse that made such an impact on him and had led to his own conversion.

During the time that Ian was at Dilston Hall, he linked up with some young people who were meeting at the home of Doctor Ian Gunn-Russell, a fine Christian doctor in Jesmond, a relatively prosperous part of Newcastle. He was a Brethren man and a great Bible teacher. He and his wife Helen had meetings in their house every other Tuesday, and a number of students and young people would meet in their sitting room. There would be lots of informative discussion and because Ian Gunn-Russell knew the Bible very well, he could answer their questions.

In 1957 Ian was again looking for work. It was through the amazing grace of God that his mentor Ian Gunn-Russell was in the process of building a house and surgery in Longbenton. At that time, practices grew by establishing branch surgeries out from the city in the new estates and suburbs. Longbenton was one of those new estates built to serve the overspill areas of Newcastle. The new house was to be a branch of Ian Gunn-Russell's Jesmond practice, and he offered Ian the job in Longbenton. The decision to accept the job formed the basis of the next phase of Ian's life and the house became his home for the following thirty years.

Ian was very grateful for the blessings provided through Ian Gunn-Russell. In Ian's own words, *"He had a huge impact on our lives, helping us grow in Christ, providing me with a job and a house and being part of the way God brought Helen and me together."* We shall see how he and Helen were brought together in the next chapter.

Chapter Two
Helen

Ian's and Helen's lives became very much intertwined through the meetings held in the home of Ian Gunn-Russell and his wife Helen. They had, however, known each other before, going back some ten years. Ian's Aunt Lillian acted as a matchmaker by pairing them together for the Church High School Old Girls' Dance in 1947. Ian later invited Helen to the May Ball in Cambridge and they also met in London. Ian, however, decided at this stage that Helen was not the girl for him.

Helen had always had a longing to become a nurse but had been persuaded to follow a more academic route. She therefore applied to study history (strangely, the subject that Ian was originally going to study before God told him otherwise) in Oxford and London, but unfortunately was not offered a place. She ended up taking a secretarial course in Eastbourne, and then obtained a post as a secretary at the BBC.

The longing to do nursing, however, remained, and she gave up her job in London and came home ready to proceed to Edinburgh to train for four years as a nurse. For Helen it was a daunting step, and she confided in her mother about her fears. Her mother told her that some people open up the Bible and put a pin in a verse to get guidance. Although this approach to obtaining God's guidance is not generally to be recommended, God was at work and the verse they hit was from the book of Ruth, *"Go, my daughter."*[2] Helen followed

---

2   Ruth 2:2 (Authorised Version)

this word, and started her training in Edinburgh at the age of twenty-one. Her training was hard going, but she went on to love nursing. Her secretarial experience would not be wasted, however, as she would be able to use it along with her nursing qualification in the practice in Longbenton.

During her nursing training, Helen became a Christian through the leading of her brother Robin Nixon. He himself had become a Christian along with a number of other scholars while studying at Winchester College. Robin went into the ministry, and so was later able to help officiate at their wedding. Ultimately he became principal of St John's College in Nottingham, but tragically died in his forties.

When Helen came back home to Newcastle to add to her nursing qualifications, she too attended the meetings at the home of the Gunn-Russells, where she caught glimpses of Ian Longfield who now began to realise that Helen might in fact be the girl for him after all. As he himself put it, *"Now we were both Christians and were medically trained, and were meeting in the home of this lovely Christian couple. What more appropriate than to go forth together?"*

As Ian and Helen looked back on those days in 1957 through the lens of over sixty years of happy marriage, they admit that they cannot remember all the events, thoughts and feelings of the time. They do, however, recall that being together at a conference in Filey was very significant. Helen remembers travelling there on the train from Newcastle with a Christian couple who also knew Ian. They asked her who would be at the conference that she knew. When she mentioned Ian, they exchanged knowing glances, though she was not aware of the growing interest that Ian had in her. This interest led him to ensure that they were in the same groups and were able to spend time together. Ian recalls that it was there he decided that he wanted to ask Helen to marry him. It was a decision he has had no cause to regret.

There was, however, an issue that they had to resolve in that Helen had answered a missionary appeal at Filey and had expressed her willingness to serve God overseas. She already had experience and training in midwifery and tropical diseases, and was in the process of increasing her theatre experience as a staff nurse at the Royal Victoria Infirmary in Newcastle. As Helen herself recollected:

I felt that I should stand and express my willingness to go abroad. However, Ian already felt that God was not calling him abroad, partly because of his eye condition. We were at the point of thinking about getting engaged and my response to the call to go abroad created some uncertainty for us. As a result we decided, on returning from Filey, not to meet for a fortnight while I sought God and asked what to do. The verse that I was given as I read the Bible came from Ezekiel, where God says to the prophet, "For thou art not sent to a people of a strange speech and of a hard language, but to the house of Israel."[3] In other words, Ezekiel was being sent to his own people. This gave me a measure of peace and encouraged us to go ahead.

It is fascinating how God spoke to each separately and in different ways before either became a Christian. He gave each the help they needed in a way that they could understand and accept. He led Helen to pursue the nursing that he had already put on her heart, and he spoke to Ian about medicine, a career that he had not ever considered, when he called to the Lord for help. Although they had met many years earlier, now having been brought to Jesus and having a similar calling to medicine, the dynamic was different; Jesus was at the centre of their lives.

---

3 Ezekiel 3:5 (Authorised Version)

Ian and Helen's Wedding

Their wedding day on February 8th 1958 was a very special day for them, but it could so easily have gone wrong. Very heavy snow fell overnight and covered all the streets of Newcastle, making it very difficult for guests to travel to the ceremony. They had asked a friend of theirs, the vicar of Newburn who was a very evangelical churchman, to marry them but he was not able to get there, and so the local vicar (whom they had originally bypassed) very graciously conducted the ceremony, assisted by Helen's brother, Robin. The organist and official photographer were not able to get there either. There were no wedding cars, and so they all had to use taxicabs. The reception was booked for Gosforth Racecourse and fortunately the clerk of the racecourse had been invited to the wedding, so he got the snow cleared from the racecourse. They were very happy that Ron Pont, Ian's friend from Cambridge, was there as best man.

Their honeymoon adventures started after the wedding. They were unable to drive to Edinburgh because of the snow, and so they spent their first night together at the White Swan Hotel in Alnwick. The following day they were able to travel on to Edinburgh and then to Pitlochry but, because of the snow, the bride had to push the car for the final stretch up the hill to reach the Pine Trees Hotel.

Helen was the ideal partner for Ian in all of his years of service. Whereas Ian was very much a leader, Helen was an excellent second-in-command. The people of Longbenton were very pleased when the young doctor who had moved in to live on the estate came back with a young wife. Together they would influence the lives of many as they lived and worked amongst them.

One of the hymns they sang at their wedding was "Take My Life and Let it Be", the famous nineteenth-century hymn of consecration written by Frances Ridley Havergal. At this very special event, Ian and Helen were not only committing themselves to each other but also to the Lord as they started out on their life journey together.

As they undertook God's work in Longbenton, Ian and Helen discovered the truth of God's words in Proverbs:

> *Trust in the* LORD *with all your heart*
> *and lean not on your own understanding;*
> *in all your ways submit to him,*
> *and he will make your paths straight.*[4]

God had put his hand firmly on their lives, placed them in the careers that he wanted them to follow, brought them together as husband and wife, and settled them in that pàrt of his vineyard where they were to serve him. They would continue to find God going before them in the years to come.

---

4 Proverbs 3:5-6

Chapter Three
Establishing a Practice

As we have already seen, during Ian's training he was very conscious that a number of his Christian medical friends were planning to follow God's calling to serve him abroad by working in poor communities in less developed countries. They were going to live amongst the people they were serving, and thus live out their Christian lives before them. Because of his eyesight, Ian knew that he was restricted to practising medicine in the United Kingdom, but he was determined to live in the community in which he was working, Longbenton.

Building up the Practice

Ian Gunn-Russell's vision coincided with Ian Longfield's. He had come from a business family, and was very much an entrepreneur and businessman as well as a very good doctor. He saw the potential for establishing a viable practice from scratch in Longbenton and recognised this as an opportunity to bring the gospel to the community there. He decided to buy one of three plots of land that were available and, because he got in first, was able to buy the one that was on the main road. He organised the building of the surgery whilst looking for a young Christian doctor to establish the branch of the practice in Longbenton, living in the surgery house. Ian Longfield was of course that young Christian doctor who would spearhead the work in Longbenton. Furthermore, the choice to "live on the patch" was a conscious decision on Ian's part.

Just prior to this, Ian Gunn-Russell had appointed Donald Gascoigne in a similar way to a surgery on Brunton Park in the outskirts of Newcastle. Ian Longfield had great respect for Donald, who was a highly principled and excellent physician. The three doctors had different areas of responsibility but worked well together.

Ian Longfield's natural leadership abilities came to the fore in developing the work in the practice and on the estate. He had always been seen as a leader. At school he was head boy and captain of the cricket team. Likewise, Ian Gunn-Russell also saw the leadership potential that Ian Longfield clearly had and entrusted the work of the practice in Longbenton to him.

Ian brought that leadership ability, together with his understanding of propagating the gospel through service, to his work in Longbenton. He explained it as follows:

> *There was always a Christian component in what I was doing in the working world, and so when we came to Longbenton I was aware that there would be a Christian aspect to the work there. I wasn't sure what it would be but it was certainly there at the back of my mind. And having a vision for this, I was able to bring others along into what we started to do. They brought and used their gifts in the context and through the opportunities that our initiatives brought.*

The Longbenton branch, under Ian, was seeking to build up the practice from very small foundations. It was not easy as when they first moved there facilities were very primitive and the practice was in effect really Ian on his own, with no nurse, receptionist or other staff. At the beginning, the medical cards of all the registered patients fitted into a couple of shoe boxes. They had about a hundred patients on the estate but needed many more to be viable. It took drive and committed hard work.

For most of the time Helen needed to be in the house when Ian was out. Her nursing training also meant that she was able to help with some of the medical and health issues of those who came to the surgery out of hours. There were no appointments and people used to come to the door to arrange for Ian to call or to join the practice. As Helen recalled, *"In this way I got to know people. The local people were very friendly, and if I was cleaning my windows they would ask me if I could come and do theirs later."* Likewise, because the surgery was in their home and Ian was making regular home visits, it was easier for the community to relate to the doctor.

Ian and Helen were very generous with their time and the resources that they had in their home. They cared very much for the people who lived on the estate. As Ian walked around the estate, he would ask the patients he met how they were getting on, and as he visited them in their homes, he was able to take an interest in the whole family. He was always concerned for them and friendly towards them, getting to know many of them well; to Ian they were far from being faceless people on a list.

Ian and Helen had a particular heart for those with greater needs and went out of their way to help them, be they patients or not. Indeed if someone who was particularly unwell needed a place to recuperate, Ian and Helen would occasionally invite them to stay in their home for a short time. People could so easily have taken advantage of their kindness, but this did not happen; rather they won the respect of the local residents. This highly committed approach to caring for the people of the estate continued for over thirty years.

The practice was very much a Christian practice during Ian's time of leadership, with God being at the centre of their work. Many of the staff appointed over that period were Christians, and so those working in the practice had a very similar ethos. Prayer was key to the operation. Ian started each day in the surgery with prayer, involving whoever was there at the time. There was a prayer board in the surgery, unseen by the general public, with the names of those who needed urgent prayer for their illnesses, as well as the names of those who had died so that their families could be prayed for. Biblical texts were openly on display in the surgery, and indeed representatives from pharmaceutical companies who visited the surgery called it "the church". John McKale, now a member of the leadership team at New Life Church in Morpeth, remembered how as a Christian young man living on the Longbenton estate in the 1960s he would go to the surgery for a routine appointment. *"The surgery was full of people, but Doctor Longfield would spend twenty minutes with me and then pray. He was a great encourager."*

Ken and Rosie Prudhoe were patients of Ian in Longbenton in the 1970s, and appreciated the godly care that he gave them in their early married life. Rosie recollects:

As a GP, Ian immunised our children and was always available when I panicked about various childhood problems. One thing that I will always be grateful for is that he never tried to "spiritualise" problems that were actually psychological. Having experience of working in psychiatry meant that he dealt with these in a very professional way. Even after we moved away in 1981, I was able to call him in times of real difficulty and trust him for wise, godly advice.

Ken himself undertook medical training from 1974 to 1979 with a view to becoming a general practitioner. Ken believes that Ian provided him with a role model *"for combining professional medical practice with Christian witness in a local community".*

In 1961 Ian's mentor Ian Gunn-Russell had felt led by the Lord to move away from Newcastle to his home city of Edinburgh with his wife Helen and his children. Here they would be involved not only in medicine, but also in establishing a Christian retreat centre. The practice was left in the hands of Donald Gascoigne and Ian. Edinburgh was not too far from Newcastle, and so it was not too difficult for the Longfields and Gunn-Russells to keep in touch. To Ian and Helen's surprise and sadness, however, the Gunn-Russells moved much further afield in 1983 when they emigrated to New Jersey in the United States to join the fellowship where their son-in-law was one of the pastors.

There was a certain "old-world" charm about the operation of the practice as run by Donald and Ian which, to those trained as general practitioners in the 1970s and 1980s, could at times be seen to be very frustrating. One such practitioner was Valerie Wadge who as a young Christian doctor joined the practice in January 1983. She found Ian and Donald to be, using her own words, *"very conscientious clinicians, but out of date (I am sure that Ian wouldn't mind me saying that); they gave good patient care, but they were not so good at making forward plans".* Part of the problem was that Valerie was a new breed of GP who had received formal postgraduate general practitioner training, which had been introduced into the profession in 1976, whereas this was not a requirement for Donald's and Ian's generation. More significant perhaps was the fact that Donald found any kind of change very challenging, and understandably wanted to continue the operation of the practice as he had always known it. He did the bookkeeping for the practice himself, for example, and wrote all of his letters by hand until he retired, despite having a receptionist who had experience as a medical secretary and who could have typed his letters for him.

Valerie felt that Ian could see the need for change but, in her view, *"he did not like conflict at all; he was a peacemaker"*. Ian would often get Valerie to soft pedal a bit while he tried to negotiate with Donald. He was very much a mediator, not wanting to curb the youthful enthusiasm of his new colleague, but at the same time not wanting to cause his old partner undue stress. In so doing, he was able to temper Valerie's enthusiasm without squashing it. A number of changes did, however, take place as a result of Valerie's prompting.

Despite the fact that there were frustrations for Valerie in the practice, she did learn a lot from Ian. He had a wealth of knowledge, not only about medicine but also about his patients and their families over several generations. He also had the wisdom of knowing how to manage people and difficult situations, including when it was appropriate to pray for patients.

Sue Glover was one of the receptionists who worked in the practice, starting in November 1988, by which time Ian had reduced his hours and he and Helen had moved out of the surgery house to their own home in Melton Park in Newcastle. Although Ian was now working part-time, Sue felt that his influence was still very much present in the practice. She saw the great love that Ian and Helen had for the residents of the estate, and the fact that they constantly looked out for the vulnerable. There was a good working atmosphere amongst the staff who it seemed, in her words, *"were all singing from the same hymn sheet"*. Sadly, however, after Ian left the practice in 1992, it became, according to Sue, *"much less Christian focused"*, as the policy changed to appoint staff who were not necessarily Christians. Ultimately they were not allowed to display Christian posters and leaflets in case they caused offence.

A Missional Community in Longbenton

God was beginning to establish through the service of Ian and Helen the foundations of a missional community. Todd Engstrom, an American pastor, gives the definition of a missional community as *"a community of Christians, on mission with God, in obedience to the Holy Spirit, who demonstrate the gospel tangibly and declare the gospel creatively to a pocket of people"*.[5] At the beginning of his work in general practice, Ian knew that that was what he was called to do in Longbenton, although at that stage, he did not yet know how it was going to be worked through.

He knew, however, that things were falling into place and he put it this way:

> *God brought different things together: my own background among doctors who were going abroad to serve; my wife, ready to come to Longbenton, and with experience through her nursing of relating to different kinds of people; a vacancy in a practice run by a Christian doctor who has a business and evangelistic vision for the estate; and my own eye condition, to start this community.*

Ian could see that what was being established was all of God. Although God does not inflict sickness upon us, he even allowed Ian's eye condition to be used as part of his overall plan for Longbenton, as it prevented Ian from working abroad. As Paul says so encouragingly in his letter to the Romans, *"And we know that in all things God works for the good of those who love him, who have been called according to his purpose."*[6]

---

5   https://www.thegospelcoalition.org/article/what-makes-a-missional-community-different/
6   Romans 8:28

Reflecting on their experience, Ian was able to say:

Looking back at our lives in Longbenton we really feel that we were given the pattern of a missional community on a plate. It was just the natural expression of deciding to live on the estate. I was the doctor in a practice that was just starting and needed to recruit patients, the family was brought up there, and, once the shops were built, Helen shopped there. In these ways, but particularly through the surgery and visiting patients' homes, we related to the local people and got to know them. It was a natural part of our lives and the living out of what today might be called a missional community.

In his Sermon on the Mount, Jesus gave these instructions to his followers:

You are the light of the world. A town built on a hill cannot be hidden. Neither do people light a lamp and put it under a bowl. Instead they put it on its stand, and it gives light to everyone in the house. In the same way, let your light shine before others, that they may see your good deeds and glorify your Father in heaven.[7]

This is exactly what Ian and Helen were doing; they were letting their light shine for Jesus as they lived and worked on the estate, building up relationships and ultimately pointing people to the Lord.

What was yet to come, however, was the establishment of Christian activities on the estate flowing out from the life of the surgery.

---

7 Matthew 5:14-16

Chapter Four
Establishing a Church in the Community

Ian's surgery grew as the estate grew and as he and Helen established relationships with the local people. They both realised that there was a great spiritual need on the estate, and they sought the Lord as to the next steps to begin to meet that need. People needed to hear about Jesus and commit their lives to him.

They were fortunate to be joined in this by other Christian people with whom Ian was able to share his vision. Two of those who became deeply involved in the work and who became very close friends of Ian and Helen over the forthcoming decades were Lester and Margaret Morgan. They lived in nearby Gosforth but had a heart for Longbenton, and worked in partnership with Ian and Helen in all the different Christian activities on the estate.

Sunday School

Ian recalled standing on the path of the surgery talking to Ian Gunn-Russell not long after he had started in Longbenton and commenting on the signs that had been erected at both ends of the estate requesting people to drive carefully as there were four thousand children living on the estate. That was a massive number, but that was commonplace on housing estates in the 1950s. After the war there was a great housing shortage, and these new council housing estates around Newcastle provided welcome first homes for many young couples with their children born since the end of the war.

There was such a potential harvest here that it was clear they should start a Sunday school. Ian was able to have, free of charge, the use of the hall and classrooms of Somervyl School in the middle of the estate. On the first Sunday afternoon, they welcomed 250 children who flooded into the school. Numbers stabilised at 150 for several years. There was a good team of workers, comprising a mixture of friends (some from Central Hall in Elswick) and students who wanted to help. Ian took charge of the overall event, while Helen looked after the children of the teachers.

Sunday school was fun for both the teachers and the children. Each summer, the children and some of their parents were taken on trips to the coast. In the early years, this involved hiring double-decker buses or even a train. There was one instance when they accidentally brought back an extra child on the train; the child realised that he had got off at the wrong station with the wrong party and had then to be taken by car to Wallsend. These trips were important in cementing relations between the teachers, the children and their families; a game of cricket with Ian demonstrating his prowess as a sportsman helped to get the Christians alongside the families who came on these trips.

The work of the Sunday school provided Ian and all the helpers with a great deal of respect in the community. An interest in the gospel was evident and led to some parents making commitments to follow Jesus.

One example of this was the way in which the Lord worked within the Warren family who lived on the estate. As a young boy, Simon was sent by his mum and dad to the Sunday school, initially in Somervyl School and then later in the chapel once it had been built. Simon heard that there was a need for a pianist to play in the chapel services, and so he asked his mum, Miriam, if she would go along to play the piano. She agreed and as a result she became a Christian and, soon afterwards, his dad was also converted. Simon himself made a commitment to the Lord in his Sunday school days. In Simon's own words, *"Our family was dramatically changed as a result of the Longfields."*

Simon, however, drifted away from the Lord through his teens and early twenties, but the fellowship continued to pray for him and, despite all of his rebellion, the Lord continued to have his hand upon him. Ian played a key role in bringing Simon back to a relationship with the Lord by lending him Martyn Lloyd-Jones' classic exposition of Romans chapter 1.[8] Simon worked through the text and realised that Paul's description of depraved humanity was a true description of his own sinful state. Simon wanted to read more and bought for himself Lloyd-Jones' exposition of chapters 3 and 4.[9] He was particularly struck by how God's righteousness was manifested to us through Jesus and although we all sin and fall short of the glory of God, we can be made righteous by God's grace. This was only possible through the sacrifice of his blood that Jesus made for us on the cross.[10] For Simon this was the turning point, and he recommitted his life to the Lord. Jesus was now at the centre of his life, and Simon worked alongside Ian and others over the next few years in the chapel.

The Ladies' Meeting

Soon after the Sunday school had got underway, some of the ladies working with Ian and Helen decided that they would like to have a Christian meeting for ladies on a Monday night. They were very definite that it would be a place where ladies could learn from the Bible and pray and worship together, and it would not turn into a

---

8   Martyn Lloyd-Jones, *Romans: An Exposition of Chapter 1 – The Gospel of God* (Banner of Truth, 1973).

9   Martyn Lloyd-Jones, *Romans: An Exposition of Chapters 3:20 – 4:25 – Atonement and Justification* (Banner of Truth, 1970).

10 Romans 3:21-26

cookery or a sewing class. The meetings were held in the same school that was used for the Sunday school and, although the group struggled a bit initially, they were able to keep it going and it gradually built up over the years. The normal attendance was in the twenties, but on one occasion there were as many as eighty-four ladies present.

Miss Waugh, a former missionary who joined the fellowship for some time, helped them in this. She visited all the homes in the new fifteen-storey blocks of flats that had been built in Longbenton, and through her visitation a number of ladies came to the ladies' meeting and became Christians. The group would often have visiting speakers, and some of them had a very powerful effect; Helen remembered John Rowling and John McKale in particular as being very gifted evangelists and a number of ladies made professions of faith when they spoke at the meeting.

Establishing Somervyl Chapel

By this time, Ian and Helen, along with their young family, David, Jane and Sally, had left Central Hall in Elswick to concentrate on the work in Longbenton. They held a Sunday morning service in their home attended by several local people as well as those friends who were involved in helping them with the work on the estate. About twenty to thirty people came to the meetings that were held in their upstairs lounge, although with growing numbers, it was beginning to overflow down the stairs!

Iris Bell, one of the members of the ladies' meeting, was very persistent in saying to Ian that they should hold a meeting for men, and indeed even build a church. Ian was initially a bit reluctant to move forward with the idea of a brand-new building as it would be a huge project and involve considerable expense. Iris prevailed, however, and stimulated by the overflowing numbers in the house meeting, Ian and others started to plan.

Ian led the negotiations with Northumberland County Council who owned the land and Newcastle Housing who managed the housing stock. They were allocated a very suitable piece of land, a good open space not far from the surgery and close to two fifteen-storey blocks of flats. Members of the group working with Ian and Helen gave generously, as did other Christian individuals and organisations to whom they sent appeal letters. One individual who gave a generous personal gift was Doctor Martyn Lloyd-Jones from Westminster Chapel in London. He had inspired Ian by his preaching and teaching when he was training in London, and Ian, never one to miss an opportunity, approached Doctor Lloyd-Jones when he was preaching at Brunswick Methodist Church in the centre of Newcastle. He was pleased to receive a sizeable cheque in the post not long afterwards. The gifts mounted up, and they were able to pay for the building without at any stage getting into debt.

Ian and a small group of other members visited newly built churches both locally and in Scotland to get ideas. Mike Jeffrey, an architect friend of Ian's from Edinburgh, offered his services and arranged for a local supervisor and builders to take on the project.

God had brought all these people together to build what was a fine, modern church building for the estate. Ian was overwhelmed by the response to the project saying very thankfully, *"I must record my gratitude to those, many of whom have passed on to glory, for all of their faith, work and sacrifice, which enabled the chapel to be built."*

God was very much going to bless the work that he had started.

Chapter Five
Blessings in Abundance

The Early Days of Somervyl Chapel

Somervyl Chapel was opened on Saturday, September 2nd 1967. It was a great day. There was a full house and it was a very happy occasion. The day was well supported by local churches as well as people from the estate with whom they were already in contact. Ian welcomed everyone and had the opportunity to thank all those who had helped in many different ways. The preacher that day was Don Bridge who was at that time pastor of Blakelaw Evangelical Church in Newcastle.

On the following day the chapel had its first service, with about sixty people attending. John Rowling, a maths teacher at the Newcastle Royal Grammar School, came and preached the gospel message in the evening. John was a brilliant schoolteacher who would later become a headteacher and be knighted for his services to education. He was also a gifted evangelist, and many were converted when John preached.

One lady who came that evening and had her life transformed was Lily. Ian recounted her story:

She was a very bitter and unhappy lady who lived in the flats almost opposite our house. She looked down from her flat and would see me going to post my letters in the box on the corner of Stoneleigh Avenue. She would think, "I don't like that prig of a man." She lived with her family but was very bitter such that she had thrown her wedding ring across the floor when her husband had died. One of the girls in the family, who was about ten years old, attended the Sunday school and it was she who brought Lily (whom she called Granny) along to that first Sunday evening service. She came and sat right in the front row under the preacher's nose. I am not sure how much of John's powerful sermon Lily really understood, but when John asked anyone who wanted to be a Christian to put their hand up, Lily put her hand up. When she was on the way out of the service, John spotted her and asked her to come to the vestry where he led her to Jesus. After that day she came to every morning service, every evening service, and every Wednesday mid-week meeting. She also joined the cleaning rota and she scrubbed the floors on her knees. What an amazing transformation we saw in her life. During those days we used to go out on sunny evenings in the summer to sing hymns in the street. It was a number of years later when the folks were saying their goodbyes after the hymn singing, that one of the congregation said, "See you on Wednesday evening at the Bible study, Lily," to which she replied, "I don't think so." She died that Tuesday: a wonderful story of a remarkable lady.

Soon after the building was opened, the church had a crusade lasting ten days in 1968 led by John Dyer, a youth evangelist. This was a time of great blessing when God very clearly spoke to many people, both young and old, who committed their lives to the Lord. John was a very able preacher who, with his racy style and sense of humour, appealed to people of all ages.

One lady who became a Christian through John's preaching was Marion. Ian recalled her story:

Marion was a very fine lady who lived on the fourteenth floor of a fifteen-storey block of flats from where she overlooked the church as it was being built. She said to herself, "When that church opens I am going to go there." And she did. Then when John Dyer was running his crusade in May she had by that time been attending for about six months. On the last Monday after the packed-out main gospel meeting was over, John decided to have an after-meeting in the back hall. It was at that meeting that Marion stood up and gave her life to Christ. She was totally committed and became a powerful and loving woman of God. She taught in the Sunday school, was very involved in the ladies' meeting and served as a deacon. She used to say, "Expect a miracle every day, expect a miracle when you pray." And this amazing woman of God, this lovely lady, used to go out each day with that expectation of a miracle in her heart. She was a wonderful witness on the estate. Sadly she developed cancer and died about six years later. But before that, her daughter also became a Christian. At different times, both Marion and her daughter worked as receptionists in my Longbenton surgery. Marion was the only receptionist I ever had who was able to, not quite tick me off, but say to me, "I don't think that you did that quite right, Doctor."

The church was very keen for John to stay on as pastor, but he felt called to serve a church in the Manchester area. It would be another three years before the church was able to find a suitable man to be taken on as pastor. During that time, Ian and other members of the fellowship took on some of the preaching responsibilities themselves; Ian's sermons were very much appreciated and, in the words of one of the members, Ken Prudhoe, *"consistently biblical and practical"*. In fact, the local people called the chapel "Longfield's Chapel" because

Ian was so well known in the local community and he was clearly associated with the leadership of the fellowship. Indeed, there was even a telephone extension in the chapel so that if anybody needed Ian's services as a doctor, they could phone him there if he was not at home.

A number of preachers came to speak at the chapel from elsewhere. Some of these men were local but some came from further afield, and a number were serving missionaries. Both the Longfields and their close friends the Morgans provided hospitality for visitors to the chapel who required a bed for the night or meals during their visits. Although it was hard work providing hospitality, they saw it very much as a privilege.

Pastor David Hollinshead

In 1971 the church was able to appoint a pastor named David Hollinshead on the recommendation of Lester Morgan who was church secretary. At first David lived in a flat near the chapel but, after he got married to Jenny and had two sons, the church bought a house for them. David was a fine Christian and a good preacher. He took a great interest in the estate and was well liked by the residents. It was a time of fruit under his leadership and ministry.

Ian was very supportive towards David and encouraged others to be so, even if they did not always agree with the pastor's decision. Despite the church being known as "Longfield's Chapel", he believed in allowing the pastor to get on with his job without unnecessary interference from him.

David was a man who knew the importance of prayer and he established a Tuesday early-morning prayer meeting which continued for many years. Prayer was part of the fabric of the chapel. A special prayer time was called when Julie, a sixteen-year-old daughter of

Elsie, one of the church members, developed acute leukaemia. At the time, there was no cure and no hope. David visited Julie in hospital, and also Elsie at home. A previously almost untested treatment was offered as a last hope and, as a result of this treatment and all of the prayer backing behind it, Julie is still alive today as a happy grandmother, for which Elsie gives the Lord all the praise.

Children's work through the Sunday school and other activities continued to attract lots of youngsters who looked for fun and enjoyment, and who were prepared to listen to the gospel. Dave Glover, an evangelist supported by the church and part of the leadership team, played a major role in coordinating the activities for children. Whereas many churches organise week- or perhaps fortnight-long holiday clubs throughout the summer holidays, Dave ran a holiday club morning and afternoon over the full six weeks of the holidays. He and his helpers had great stamina, and they saw lots of fruit for their efforts.

Church members regularly visited the residents in the flats and houses around the chapel. These visits sought to meet the people where they were, share the love of God with them and invite them to the many activities or groups that were running in the chapel. The church ran a mum-and-toddler group, a children's programme during the week called the "Hour of Discovery", and took services in a couple of the local senior citizens' homes. To try to help the local employment situation in a practical way, the church ran the "Carpenter's Shop", where some of those without work on the estate were given the opportunity to learn new employment skills. They organised food parcels after the big harvest thanksgiving services, and had open-air singing and preaching, often led by Dave Glover, outside the chapel and at the shops.

It had to be said that not all of the church's evangelistic efforts went well. The Don Summers' crusade of June 1980 held in a large tent on the green at the back of the surgery in Longbenton (which had to be guarded by church members over night) was not very well attended or very fruitful.

David Hollinshead carried on a very effective ministry until unfortunately his health began to fail. Sadly, David had a deformed spine and was not physically very strong. Ian encouraged him for some time but, as his doctor, he realised that David was no longer able to fulfil his role, and the church had to cease his employment in 1983. David was very gracious and accepted that he could not continue in his employment with the church. Ian helped him and the family to settle in Colin Urquhart's Kingdom Faith retreat centre in Sussex until, about a year later, at still a young age, David passed away.

Pastor Mark Sharman

Almost immediately after David left, Mark Sharman came through the influence of Bob Gordon, a member of staff at Kingdom Faith where Mark had been working for a short time. Mark, his wife Sandy and their young family spent a week getting to know the church members and enjoying their hospitality before Mark took up his new position in Easter 1983. They all soon settled into the life of the church. Ian recalled:

Following his coming we had some exciting times. We had some very happy, enjoyable, fruitful and profitable years under his leadership. I remember his Bible studies; a full back hall with lots of people coming from other places on a Wednesday night to hear this dynamic young man who was teaching. He built on the excellent work that David Hollinshead had started and the church continued to grow. These were very, very good days.

People were converted through Mark's ministry. Ian remembered one lady in particular, Sophie, and her husband Ernest:

Sophie was a patient in the Freeman Hospital. Although she did not really know him personally she sent for our pastor, Mark Sharman. As she was unwell she wanted someone to visit her. He did so and led her to Christ. She was discharged and about six months later she wanted to be baptised. There were about five or six who were being baptised that evening and Mark had them standing in a line. He said that before we baptised them in water he was going to pray for them to be baptised in the Holy Spirit. He prayed for each one and then came to Sophie, who was last in the line. Ernest, Sophie's husband, was standing beside her, and when Mark prayed for Sophie, Ernest amazingly experienced the power of the Holy Spirit within him. Ernest had been known in Longbenton as the man who picked up "fag ends" from the street to roll his own cigarettes. As a new Christian, he himself was later baptised and, together with Sophie, was a part of the house group that we ran in our home.

Freedom in the Gospel

Ian himself during these years had great freedom to witness to his patients about his faith. Mark Sharman described him as *"brilliant at inviting his patients to church, and as a result there were so many contacts in the church that came through the surgery"*. As a Christian GP then, he had a freedom to talk to his patients about the Lord and pray with them in a way that could well get Christian medical practitioners into difficulty today. Ian shared about one patient, Sidney.

Sidney was a man in his late forties who came to church occasionally. I remember him standing at the back in some evening services. He had cancer of the lung. Medicine was so different in those days. Life was so different that I can hardly believe what it was like then. He was ultimately at home bedridden and I used to go along each evening, whether I was on call or not, and give him a morphine injection. I would have a little reading from my Living Bible, pray with him and give him the injection.

At this time, we had a couple of great friends of ours staying with us, John and Elsie Harris. They were mighty people of God who had been missionaries in Nepal, where they had been imprisoned for a month for preaching the gospel. They had also worked in Africa. While they were staying, I invited John to join me on my rounds because then I used to visit a number of patients in their homes. He came with me and when we went to see Sidney that evening I introduced him as a missionary from Africa who was staying with me. This provoked Sidney to ask why he did that, why he was a missionary. I remember John standing at the bedside replying, "God has done so much for me, and I love him so much that I can't do enough for him. I just love to serve him." That really pricked Sidney's heart and he gave his life to Christ then. I continued to go to see Sidney each evening for the last few weeks before he died. We'd have our little reading kneeling at the bedside. His wife and eldest son joined us sometimes. I conducted the funeral. I was able to do things then that might not be possible now, but God was at work through them.

Ian also had the liberty on occasion to direct patients to seek Christian healing. A most notable example of this took place in 1977 and was included in an article in the *British Medical Journal* taken from the presidential address given by Rex Gardner to the Newcastle and Northern Counties Medical Society.[11] It was also reported on the front page of the *Newcastle Evening Chronicle*.[12] Ian recalled it as follows:

> *We had a family on the estate who were patients, and whose young boy had a horrible condition called fibrosing alveolitis and was really on death's row. He was under the consultant paediatrician at the Royal Victoria Infirmary, who asked his registrar to research the disease; he found that no child under the age of one with this condition had ever recovered. The family had been told that they just had to wait for their little boy to die. The mother was in the surgery one day and I was aware that the pastor of Heaton Pentecostal Church was going to hold a healing meeting on the following Sunday, so I encouraged her to take their son and I was able to link these two up. I knew how serious the pastor was about prayer, including prayer for healing. He would have such meetings only occasionally and always prepared for them with prayer and fasting.*
>
> *So on the Sunday the whole family piled into a taxi and went to the service in the church. They sat in the front row and the baby boy was prayed for, after which there was a gradual and steady improvement. He remained under the consultant and every indication of his health gradually changed for the better, including blood tests, weight and appetite, until he was fully recovered. He is now a middle-aged man.*

---

11 Rex Gardner, "Miracles of Healing in Anglo-Celtic Northumbria as Recorded by the Venerable Bede and His Contemporaries: A Reappraisal in the Light of Twentieth-Century Experience",*British Medical Journal* (Clinical Research Edition) Volume 287, December 24th to 31st 1983, pages 1927 to 1993.

12 *Newcastle Evening Chronicle*, Tuesday, January 15th 1990.

Helen also had great freedom to tell others about Jesus. She recalls one particular case:

> *Peggy was quite notorious for having sold her son's wedding presents when he was out at work one day. One day when Peggy had something in her eye, her neighbour, Beatrice, brought her to the surgery door outside of surgery time. For some reason I brought the two ladies into the house, ended up talking about Jesus and led Peggy to the Lord there and then. Peggy had come to have her eye seen by the doctor and ended up being led to Jesus by his wife out of hours in the house. She was transformed. She had had contact with Professor Henry Pawson earlier when she had lived in the west end of Newcastle. The Christian professor of agriculture whose family had been very kind to her family must have sown some seed and God then brought her to know him through the visit to the house.*

Personal Blessings

Family life was also a source of blessing for Ian and Helen. Their three children, David, Jane and Sally, all grew up on the estate, living in the family home that housed the surgery. They took part in church activities and played with the local children, although Ian and Helen decided that they should be educated privately. Holidays were a great time of fun for the family, a time when Ian could relax with his children away from the pressures of the practice and life on the estate. He was always thinking up fun activities and games for the family to play. Easter and summer holidays in Scotland or camping as a family on the Continent were always eagerly anticipated and thoroughly enjoyed.

In due course all three were married, David to Gillian in 1986 in Somervyl Chapel, Sally to Ed in 1992, and Jane to Chris in 1997, again in Somervyl Chapel. Ian and Helen have also been very proud of their eight grandchildren, many of whom have become Christians, and of their four great-granddaughters.

Both Ian's and Helen's parents lived in Newcastle and were a great support to them, helping with the children and having all the family for Sunday dinners. When Ian's dad died suddenly at the age of sixty-two, "Gran" was left with a helper in the home but she needed and received Ian's continuing support. He visited her regularly and looked after his mum for the twenty-five years that she lived as a widow.

Later Helen's dad died at the age of seventy-nine. "Granny" lived alone for a while but they agreed that alterations should be made to the Longbenton house to create a self-contained flat for her. She came to stay and was able to live there with some support but a degree of independence. Gran's lovely help sadly retired and so Gran, too, came to stay in the family home. By now the children were adults and starting to move on, though they occasionally stayed over that period and on one occasion Sally slept on the floor under the table in Jane's room. The health of both old ladies was failing and a few months after attending David and Gill's wedding in 1986, they both passed on peacefully. That summer, Jane and Sally bought a house together, and so the full and busy Longbenton home was suddenly very quiet.

During these years, Ian and Helen grew in their knowledge of the Lord as they saw him change lives in Longbenton. They also received great encouragement from attending different conferences, including those run by Movement for World Evangelisation, Colin Urquhart's Kingdom Faith and Terry Virgo. In addition, Helen attended the local Lydia prayer group, part of the Lydia International Prayer Fellowship for women, as well as their conferences at Swanwick, both of which were a great blessing to her. These events gave them experience of different expressions of Christianity, broadened their outlook and brought them into contact with lots of different people.

There were indeed blessings in abundance. When there are blessings, however, Satan tries to disrupt the work that God is doing.

Chapter Six
Dealing with Division

As we read the book of Acts, we see the gospel going out and reaching huge numbers of people, turning the ancient world upside down. The apostle Paul saw many saved, with new churches being established and converts being built up in the Lord. He also saw disunity within these churches, with Corinth being a notable example. He condemned their "worldly approach" when he said, *"You are still worldly. For since there is jealousy and quarrelling among you, are you not worldly? Are you not acting like mere humans? For when one says, 'I follow Paul,' and another, 'I follow Apollos,' are you not mere human beings?"*[13] They were certainly not behaving as mature Christians.

Of course, even mature Christians can have disagreements. Paul and his previously loyal companion Barnabas *"had such a sharp disagreement that they parted company"*.[14] The disagreement was over whether they should take Mark with them on their next missionary expedition; Barnabas wanted to take him, but Paul did not. In the end, Barnabas took Mark, whilst Paul took Silas, and they went spreading the gospel in different directions.

The Christian church has faced divisions throughout its history from New Testament times to the present day. These divisions are often centred round disagreements over fundamental doctrine and how we interpret Scripture, or sadly whether we even bother with Scripture at all. These doctrines are what Paul calls *"of first*

13 1 Corinthians 3:3-4
14 Acts 15:39

importance".[15] Some differences may be about preferences over modes of worship, which can probably be classed as of secondary importance. Too often, however, the divisions are over prevailing personalities within a fellowship, with particular factions believing that they know best and that they are right.

Ian Hamilton, a Presbyterian minister and lecturer, likens the church to a family, and those who believe in the fundamental truths of the gospel and trust in Christ as their Saviour are part of that family, and should be accepted as such, even though they have different views on other issues. As he writes, *"Family life can be problematic, and, sadly, can be dysfunctional. But family is family no matter how problematic or dysfunctional."*[16]

Early Signs of Division

Ian, in both his leadership role within Longbenton and within the wider church on Tyneside, would agree very strongly with these words of Ian Hamilton. Indeed unity was one of Ian's three greatest desires and for which he prayed constantly, along with the desire to see people being saved in Longbenton and revival across the nation.

He was also aware that, as the church grew on the estate and the Lord gave blessings in abundance, there would be attacks on the church as Satan mobilised his forces against it. There were disagreements and even divisions over time and Ian had to be very gracious as he dealt with the issues and people involved. Ken Prudhoe, a member of the fellowship in the 1970s, remembers how Ian dealt with difficult situations.

I saw him at close quarters in various challenging church or pastoral situations, at times in shared leadership situations. He

---

15 1 Corinthians 15:3
16 Ian Hamilton, *The Gospel-Shaped Life* (Banner of Truth, 2017), page 43.

had a knack for seeing the key factors and was able to analyse complex issues succinctly and from a biblical perspective. As a result, his prayers were specific and well-aimed, and our church response was usually wise and well-directed.

Ian had the experience of seeing some of his Christian patients holding different views and expressing their faith in different ways, while each loved and sought to serve God. He was aware that, given they had different views, they could not all be right! This led to a realisation that he, too, may not be right in his understanding. Perhaps this was part of the reason why he often took a middle road in any disagreement about church practice as he sought to maintain unity. He recognised that in some ways both sides were right and in other ways perhaps both were wrong.

When people felt that they had to leave the church over some issue, it was always with much soul searching, deep sadness and very heavy hearts because Somervyl was where they had found fellowship and had served the Lord faithfully. Ian, too, felt the sadness of their loss very much in his heart, sad for the loss of friends, for the loss of unity and for what he felt would be the negative impact on the work of the gospel on Longbenton. Yet, he never felt grudges against them and now has restored positive relationships with them. He is able to say about people who had moved to worship and serve elsewhere, *"The lovely thing is that we get on very, very well with all these people; that's the wonderful thing about the church of Jesus."* He felt that this was in contrast to what happened in many other places: *"The sad thing about the church of Jesus is that when there is a split there is often animosity and the breaking of relationships, but this didn't happen at all at Somervyl."* The fact that relationships were restored is testimony to the grace demonstrated by Ian and those who left.

42

An example of this was in the early 1980s when a small group in the fellowship felt a little bit disgruntled with some aspects of David Hollinshead's ministry. This was the time when the effects of the charismatic movement were being felt in many churches, when old certainties were challenged and new expressions of worship, ministry, gifting and even leadership were coming to the fore. Some in Somervyl wanted some of these new expressions to be evident in the life of the church. Ian, however, wanted to support David, and he used a military analogy with the group by telling them that in the army the sergeant gave the commands that had to be followed and there needed to be the same discipline in the church in following the pastor. The group concerned loved David and did not want to see him hurt, but they also believed that the Lord was telling them to start up a new work in nearby Killingworth.

There were tearful discussions between Ian and members of the group. Ian felt very strongly that if these key members left, including the gifted evangelist Dave Glover, fewer people in Longbenton would be saved. The group decided to go, however, and so in 1981 they established what was to become a very fruitful work in Killingworth. There was much pain on all sides at the time, but Ian did not hold any grudges against them and sought to maintain strong relationships with them. Later he was to praise God for all the people saved in Killingworth as a result of the move from Longbenton. That was the graciousness of the man.

Likewise, those in the Killingworth fellowship who were involved at Somervyl Chapel now look back to the Longbenton days as being very formative ones for their own ministries. Dave Glover, as a church leader and evangelist, very much appreciated the support that Ian had given him and in particular the freedom to carry out his ministry with children and young people and in open-air evangelism. Peter Bentley, another of the Killingworth leaders, looked up to Ian and Helen for the inspirational way in which they worked and raised their family in the community, and saw them, as many others did, as spiritual parents.

Further Difficulties

Ian had to deal with further difficulties in the fellowship towards the end of Mark Sharman's ministry. As we have seen, under Mark there was tremendous blessing as people became Christians and grew in the Lord. The church had grown to such a size in 1989 that it was felt that it could send some of the fellowship up to the Benton area of Newcastle to the Manor Park public house that they rented for a Sunday meeting. At that point, in Ian's own words, *"things began to just go a tiny bit wrong"*.

Two men came into the fellowship about this time and very quickly became elders, which Ian admits in retrospect was a mistake. Ian himself takes responsibility for one of the appointments. With his generous heart he wanted to help a man who was a very good Bible teacher but, with hindsight, was not someone who was an appropriate leader for their fellowship. Perhaps on this occasion, Ian's heart ruled his head. In both cases, their leadership ability was not checked out beforehand and nobody in the fellowship had seen them function in a leadership role.

When it came to the move to Manor Park, Mark decided that he would go and spearhead the work there, leaving one of the new men to lead the work in Somervyl Chapel. Ian now feels that that was a mistake and, as he himself explains it:

That was a good move in one sense, but was a bad move in another, because the senior pastor went with the small group and the new pastor stayed at home to lead the church. And that was not the right thing to do, as really, the senior pastor should stay at base camp with the bulk of the congregation and another, additional person perhaps, should go and lead the plant. But that is what we did and it was perhaps a seedbed for trouble.

The church plant at Manor Park became independent in 1992, but it did not grow as they had hoped, and eventually it languished and sadly died. The closure in 1994 hit people hard, and while some of the members returned to Somervyl, others went on to other churches. Mark himself went to take up some part-time study in theology at Newcastle University, before taking up the post of pastor of Stocksfield Baptist Church in Northumberland.

Meanwhile, Somervyl itself also had difficulties, as dissatisfaction with the new leadership encouraged some people to leave. This was a very unhappy time for many in the fellowship, both for those who left and those who stayed. Ian and Helen felt very sad as many of their friends decided that they needed to move away. Those who left did so with great sadness and pain. Ian and Helen had a great deal of sympathy for them, and always wanted to maintain good relationships with them.

There are strong lessons for other churches to be learned from this experience. Great care has to be taken in appointing elders. The process has of course to be covered in prayer, but it will also include what would be normal business practice in carrying out checks as to the suitability of the individuals for the roles. Paul gave an excellent checklist to Timothy outlining the expected qualities of elders, to which churches would be wise to refer when making key appointments.[17] Likewise in establishing church plants, there has to be strong leadership in both the church at the centre and the new church plant. The main strength, however, needs to lie in the centre

17 1 Timothy 3:1-7

so that it can support the work of the plant and then establish further new plants.

The Effects of the "Toronto Blessing"

The next difficulty leading to division in the fellowship came in the mid-1990s when the "Toronto Blessing" hit the church. This was a time when many churches worldwide, starting in 1994 with the relatively small and otherwise relatively insignificant Vineyard Airport Fellowship in Toronto, seemed to have had a fresh visitation of the Holy Spirit, and many new and somewhat strange phenomena were reported. These included people being "slain in the Spirit", laughing in the Spirit and shaking uncontrollably. At the time, many testified to experiencing a greater knowledge of the presence and power of God.[18]

In the north-east, Ken Gott led renewal meetings at the Sunderland Christian Centre where the phenomena associated with the "Toronto Blessing" were experienced. Christians from fellowships, including Somervyl Chapel, went to these meetings. Blessing was experienced, but it did also lead to problems and divisions. As Ian recalls:

The church, sadly, really divided into three groups. There were those who were very keen on what was happening and who after a while said that the rest of us were a bit stuffy and were not really going for it and we ought to be going down this path with great enthusiasm. Another group said that this is not good, that this is wrong and that we ought to be pulling back from it. And there was a little group in the middle who were sort of compromising and agreeing that both were right to a certain extent and that we should go for it but with moderation. So we had in the church

---

18 A helpful analysis of the "Toronto Blessing" written at the time is given in Mike Fearnon's *A Breath of Fresh Air* (Inter Publishing Services, 1994).

three groups of people and it ended up rather sadly that these three groups divided. A group of very potentially keen people who were all for the "Toronto Blessing" went off to City Church in Newcastle and other places. Another group of more conservative people left and went and joined other churches in the traditional stream and it left a small group of us behind in the middle.

These strong differences of opinion and the divisions that resulted were painful for the church and particularly strongly felt when families who had been worshipping together were pulled apart and felt they had to go in different directions. There were friends of Ian and Helen who had worshipped and served so wholeheartedly at Somervyl for many years, but now felt they could no longer stay.

Despite the consequent splits, Ian can testify that they now have good relationships with almost all those who had left Somervyl. Relationships between other groups of Christians also appear to have been restored. Ian was able to say, *"We are still in close touch with our lovely friends who left and went to City Church, as well as the lovely people who went and joined other more conservative churches."* This was evident many years later from the large number of people who gathered together to celebrate his ninetieth birthday in October 2017; many of those who came together on that occasion were amongst those who had left Somervyl years before.

The situation that Ian and others at Somervyl found themselves in was very serious. There remained behind a small group of people who were trying to run a busy church with a lot of activities in a building with great potential. By the autumn of 1997, there were only five men left. The group felt that there were only two alternatives: either the Lord would add a few more families to enhance the number and provide a reasonable sized working group of twenty-five to thirty people, or nothing would happen and they would have to look elsewhere for someone to come and take over the church.

By the beginning of 1998, nobody else had come forward to join the fellowship, and so it was agreed that they would look elsewhere for someone to take over the church. After considering a number of possibilities to no avail, they approached Pastor Ken Gott of Bethshan Church and Revival Now. Ian recalled: *"He was willing to take us over. It was an interesting marriage and was very significant for us personally. So we gave our church over to him: the building, the church house, the money in the bank, the few people who remained and lots of prayers."*

After a period of flux with different people coming to give input and leadership, Alan and Ann Finlay, elders at Bethshan, came as the new pastors. It seemed that life had come back to Somervyl Chapel with services on Sunday mornings and with some magnificent worship meetings on Sunday evenings as crowds of young people from the other Bethshan fellowships across the region flooded into the church. Unfortunately, however, this was not to last, as Bethshan had become part of the G12 group of churches.

The Closing of Somervyl Chapel

The G12 movement began in Colombia in 1983 through the ministry of Pastor César Castellanos who used the "governance of twelve" principle to see his church grow from a group of eight meeting in his sitting room to over 150,000 members. In this model, initially twelve cell leaders are trained and they then go and disciple twelve others. One can see how this pyramid structure can lead to very fast church growth. It can, however, become a very authoritarian model, with the centre dictating very strongly how the cells should operate. The way this particularly affected Somervyl Chapel was through the decision made by Bethshan to bring all smaller congregations together; this involved closing down meetings in the chapel. Ian described this as *"a terrible blow that very sadly effectively brought the chapel as a church on the estate to an end"*. Helen also found this period to be very sad: *"When Somervyl was closed down, something in me died. We put our lives into the chapel, seeing it filled, and then seeing it empty."*

Although there was deep sadness at the closure of the chapel, Ian and Helen both took this to be part of God's greater plan, and accepted his will. They have personally stayed within Bethshan (who as a church later regretted being part of G12), and have enjoyed blessing as part of that fellowship. Ian and Helen moved off the Longbenton estate in 1988 when Ian took partial retirement from the practice, but they still have a heart for the people there and take part in prayer meetings on the estate.

Tim Dunnett, who is currently Ian and Helen's pastor at Bethshan, believes that, although Somervyl Chapel closed, there is a *"resident grace associated with the area"*. The chapel provided a temporary home for three different fellowships before they moved to their own accommodation in other parts of the city. It currently hosts a school run by the Christian charity, Transforming Lives for Good (TLG), which provides programmes for young people who are struggling in their current schools and need a more appropriate setting to help them achieve. In their most recent Ofsted inspection in February 2018 the school was judged to be good. As Tim says, *"anything in there seems to prosper"*.

God's Purposes

The divisions that took place within Somervyl Chapel over the decades were very sad for all concerned. Those who left knew that they would be losing friendships and fellowship that had been built up over many years and whatever exciting new experiences they might have in the future, there would still be a "Somervyl Chapel gap" within their lives. These wonderful friends would also, of course, be missed by those who remained.

When division occurs, there is the temptation to apportion blame to one side or the other. This, however, is not a particularly fruitful or edifying exercise. In reality, there would probably be fault on all sides and looking back, people would perhaps wish that they had done things differently. Ian would himself admit that he had not always got things right.

Ian and Helen continue to have a heart for all the people that once were part of Somervyl Chapel but who, for various reasons, left the church. They do not feel resentment towards them, but rather have allowed God's grace to shine out towards them. Their attitude was very similar to that of Paul as we mentioned at the beginning of this chapter from the story in Acts 15. Paul was saddened by the way that Mark had earlier deserted them and so did not want to take him with him on the next stage of their journeys. Although the early missionaries split up and went separate ways, positive things came out of that. First of all, there were now two teams spreading the gospel and covering different areas. Secondly, God must have worked in Mark's heart as Paul was later able to tell Timothy, *"Get Mark and bring him with you, because he is helpful to me in my ministry."*[19] Reconciliation had clearly taken place.

Division is usually very sad and hurtful but it may, on occasion, be necessary within the context of God's bigger picture. Ian would often talk about God creating a *"diverse and beautiful tapestry"*. If you look at the front of a tapestry it is a beautiful work of art, full of colour and fine detail. When you look at the back of a tapestry, however, it seems to be a hotchpotch of threads, seemingly put together with no

---

19 2 Timothy 4:11.

great purpose and certainly no beauty. Events in our lives often seem to be like the back of the tapestry; things seem to go wrong, and we do not understand the reason why, and yet the master weaver does have a purpose, which we can see when we look at the front of the tapestry. Of course, we shall see the full beauty of the tapestry when God raises us to be with him in the new heaven and new earth; then we shall fully understand the purposes of the master weaver and be in awe at what he has created.[20]

In his book *Surprised by Hope*, Professor Tom Wright explains how God uses our ministries to work out his purposes that will be manifested in his new creation. He says,

> *And of course every prayer, all Spirit-led teaching, every deed which spreads the gospel, builds up the church, embraces and embodies holiness rather than corruption, and makes the name of Jesus honoured in the world – all of this will find its way, through the resurrecting power of God, into the new creation which God will one day make.[21]*

Therefore, even when things do not work out as we had hoped, they may be used by God in a significant way through the processes and power of resurrection. The fact that Somervyl Chapel no longer exists as a functioning church does not take away from the powerful work that God did through the lives and ministries of Ian and Helen in Longbenton.

Over the decades, Ian and Helen saw lives being changed, even when it seemed that things were difficult. They learned by God's grace to deal with divisions, and to be reconciled with those who

---

20 Holocaust survivor Corrie Ten Boom who saw God at work despite all the suffering she experienced during World War II often quoted what is known as "The Tapestry Poem". It can be read in full at: https://threadofhopeorg.wordpress.com/2017/05/19/corrie-ten-boom-poem-about-suffering/
21 Tom Wright, *Surprised by Hope* (SPCK, 2007), page 219.

had gone different ways. They knew that God was sovereign and they were but one thread in his hands as he created his rich tapestry.

Chapter Seven
Developing a Wider Ministry

Prophetic Warnings

As we have seen, Ian had a heart for Longbenton, but his love for the Lord's people and for those who were lost went much wider than his local community. Ian had a burden for Tyneside, and indeed for the nation as a whole, that there might be a turning back to the Lord. As was mentioned earlier, one of his three deepest desires has been for revival. From his reading of the challenging and yet encouraging words of the Old Testament prophets, he believed that God was speaking to our nation today. For example, he was very touched by the prophecy of Joel, and this is what he felt God was saying to him about it:

> No one quite knows who Joel was, but he presented a very clear account of what was going on in Israel and Judah at that time. There had been a very severe attack of locusts on the country and that had caused great damage.[22] People were struggling through the ensuing famine and drought. The elders were told to take note and to tell their children and children's children, because nothing like this had ever happened before.[23] The land was severely assaulted and the crops and the fruit trees all dried

---

22 Joel 1:4
23 Joel 1:2-3

up and withered.[24] Even the cattle were moaning because of the lack of food and water.[25]

With the land already severely damaged, God warns them that if they do not repent there will be an even greater assault on the land with more locusts. These may be locusts, or they may be a physical human army coming.[26] So they were severely warned and told to repent and turn to God in prayer. They were to bring together elders, the priests and everybody to seek the Lord (even the nursing mothers[27] who in Judah at that time were excluded from participating in anything that first year). He warned them very severely about this. But he does say to them that if they turn to him, if they repent and if they seek his face, perhaps he will turn and change his mind.[28] That is the promise that is given.

In chapter 2 he gives amazing promises. He says, "In the last days I will pour out my Spirit on all people".[29] That wonderful quote is what Peter says on the day of Pentecost.[30] He also says that he would restore the years that the locusts have eaten.[31] There have been bad days but he will restore those days, and he also says that he who calls upon the name of the Lord will be saved.[32] There is a challenge there to true repentance, true restoration and a wonderful future.

Then it goes on in the third chapter, because perhaps we are now very near the last of the last days, to declare these climactic things that are going to happen. The prophet talks of war and

---

24 Joel 1:7
25 Joel 1:18
26 Joel 2:1-11
27 Joel 2:16
28 Joel 2:14
29 Joel 2:28
30 Acts 2:17
31 Joel 2:25
32 Joel 2:32

destruction,[33] but also blessings for the people of God.[34] The lovely thing is that there are now wonderful people who are doing a lot of excellent things in good churches and seeing a lot of fruit and a lot of blessing. But as a nation we are not fully seeing this. What our nation requires is a turning to God in a meaningful way, genuine repentance and a total restoration and blessing.

That is available to us. We are a country that has been very, very blessed by God, chosen by God and privileged by God over the years to take the gospel all over the world. The church in our nation has been tremendously used to do these wonderful things but we have rather forfeited that. There is a need for forgiveness and restoration. The challenge is in the verse that is very familiar to us all from 2 Chronicles: "If my people, who are called by my name, will humble themselves and pray and seek my face and turn from their wicked ways, then I will hear from heaven, and I will forgive their sin and will heal their land."[35] But the preceding verse says "When I shut up the heavens so that there is no rain, or command locusts to devour the land or send the plague among my people..."[36] That is a warning to us if we fail to repent and call upon the name of the Lord.

For Ian, prayer for the nation was at the heart of seeking revival. In the 1970s he had heard what had happened in Birmingham under the leadership of Bob Dunnett of the Birmingham Bible Institute. Bob and some of his colleagues began praying for their city and then felt led to pray for the nation. Furthermore, they called for the nation to pray on the first Friday of the month. That stimulated Ian to call a similar prayer meeting that was held in the Prudhoe Street Mission

---

33 Joel 3:1-16
34 Joel 3:17-21
35 2 Chronicles 7:14
36 2 Chronicles 7:13

in the middle of Newcastle. It was well attended by lots of people from across Tyneside and from different streams of churches. Over time, however, the numbers dwindled until it ended with only Ian and one lady meeting to pray, which saddened Ian enormously.

Leaders from Different Denominations

Ian also believed that it was important that Bible-believing church leaders of different persuasions should come together, forget their differences and seek the Lord for the sake of the gospel. Unity was one of the enduring passions that he had before the Lord.

Early on in his time in Longbenton, he enjoyed fellowship and working with David Smith, who from 1964 to 1968 was priest-in-charge of Saint Mary Magdalene Church, the Anglican church on the estate. David later became a bishop in the Anglican Church, including being appointed Bishop of Bradford in the 1990s. He looked back, however, to his days working on the rather tough estate of Longbenton alongside Ian as laying a strong foundation for his future ministry. David recalled that just like Somervyl, his church had need of a pianist. Whereas, as we have mentioned, it was a young Simon Warren who asked his mother to come and play the piano at Somervyl, David remembered that it was a window cleaner member of his congregation who pointed him in the direction of a young lady pianist; the window cleaner had seen lots of music certificates on the girl's bedroom wall, and so David duly approached the girl and her mother, thus solving the problem.

Because Ian's practice was seen as a Christian practice it had a disproportionate number of Christian patients, among whom were a number of leaders from a variety of different churches. In Ian's words:

I remember particularly an Elim pastor, a very exclusive Plymouth Brethren man, a reformed Anglican vicar and a lady worship leader from a local church. These people were so different, and I learned two things. The first is that not one of us has got it all right and got all the truth. This helped me to realise that I, too, am not right in everything that I think. The second is that though none of us is right in all we think and do and none has all the truth, still we are all part of God's diverse and beautiful tapestry and each has a contribution to make in and as part of God's amazing church.

As a family doctor, Ian got to know these various church leaders quite well. He was in the privileged position where they shared personal matters. He would meet their children, go to their homes and see them in their times of sickness and difficulty. For example, he had a good rapport with the different ministers in Jesmond Parish Church, a large evangelical Anglican church in Newcastle, some of whom were Ian's patients.

David Holloway, vicar of Jesmond, recalled that Ian was one of his first two visitors after he and his wife Joy had moved into the vicarage in 1973 (the other was the Bishop Designate of Newcastle, Ronald Bowlby). Ian knew of David through a common friend, David Turk, who told each of them that they ought to meet up. It only took Ian two days to come around to the vicarage. Ian was, however, at this stage probably more interested in meeting Joy, who was also a doctor, to ask her if she would like to join his practice. Joy declined as she had two young children and she also wished to be involved in paediatric work rather than general practice. David and Joy, however, did register with the practice and stayed with it until the summer of 2018, at which point they registered with a more local practice, although surprisingly they were looked after there by a former colleague of Ian, Valerie Wadge. David found Ian and his colleagues very helpful, and enjoyed the theological discussions they had together during clinical appointments.

Caring for the exclusive Brethren man demonstrated Ian's tremendous ability to get alongside Christians from completely diverse persuasions. As Ian recalled:

The Brethren man would not relate to Christians from other churches and certainly would not pray with them. He was an upstanding man of integrity, but probably felt that he had the truth and others had somehow lost it, hence the lack of relationship with those from other denominations. However, I remember praying with him. Just before I had to send his wife into hospital we knelt together at her bedside and prayed for her. As a Christian GP I had this kind of close, personal relationship with these people. It was very precious and I think it has become rarer as medical practice has changed over the years since then.

The Tyneside Leaders' Forum

Ian had a God-given desire and ability to relate to a wide range of Christians. As we have seen, it was through Ian's job that he met and related to many Christian leaders of different backgrounds. As they attended his surgery, or he visited them in their homes, he saw their faith and love for the Lord. He related to them but realised that they, perhaps, did not relate to each other. He felt that God was looking down with sadness on his people who were living and working in the same city yet barely knew each other. In his desire for unity, he longed to bring them together for the sake of the Kingdom.

In a recent radio interview, Professor Tom Wright expressed a similar view by answering the question as to what the apostle Paul would be most keen to say to us if he were to come back today. He responded as follows:

> *He would be horrified, not just that we are disunited, but that we don't care, because for Paul, the unity of the church is absolutely vital. If you are not united, why would Caesar take any notice of you? If you are not united, why would anybody believe that there really is a new creation? And so he battles for church unity across some very difficult divides all the time in every single letter.*[37]

So Paul writes to the church at Philippi, pleading for unity: *"Therefore if you have any encouragement from being united with Christ, if any comfort from his love, if any common sharing in the Spirit, if any tenderness and compassion, then make my joy complete by being like-minded, having the same love, being one in spirit and of one mind."*[38] Ian understood this, as God had given him a real passion for unity amongst Bible-believing Christians.

His good friend Mervyn Spearing pointed out the uniqueness of the opportunity Ian had to bring people together because he had the respect of, and relationships with, many Christian leaders from different denominations and persuasions from all around the region. In addition, he had been a regular visiting preacher at many churches and assemblies across the region over the years. Because he was not pastoring any particular church he had no denominational label tying him down.

Therefore, to try to bring people together, in 2004 he personally invited about one hundred Christian leaders from a variety of denominations across Tyneside to a meeting that he held in the Mansion House in Jesmond. Over fifty came, leaders who were *"part*

---

37 *Ask NT Wright Anything*, Premier Christian Radio, May 21st 2019.
38 Philippians 2:1-2

of God's diverse and beautiful tapestry", and Ian shared his vision for the group. He spoke on Psalm 133, which begins by proclaiming, *"How good and pleasant it is when God's people live together in unity!"*[39], a most apt verse to call Christian leaders of different persuasions to come and share fellowship in the Lord's name.

This short psalm continues by describing the effect of this unity in the Lord. *"It is like precious oil poured on the head, running down on the beard, running down on Aaron's beard, down on the collar of his robe."*[40] This oil is of great value and produces a wonderful fragrance for the Lord, even when it is poured on otherwise unattractive people.

This unity provides a miraculous, supernatural bonding together of very different people, pictured in the psalm as *"It is as if the dew of Hermon were falling on Mount Zion."*[41] Mount Hermon is a high mountain in the north of Israel, whereas Mount Zion is a much smaller mountain in the south, and as such they are very different. The psalmist is saying that unity provides miraculous blessings like dew being spread from different mountains far apart from each other. God's people can then know in Zion that *"the Lord bestows his blessing, even life for evermore"*.[42]

This inaugural meeting of the Tyneside Leaders' Forum was greatly appreciated by those who came. Ian had previously formed a committee consisting of key church leaders from across the evangelical spectrum, and they met regularly at his home. This group planned a programme of meetings to be held twice a year, with a variety of speakers, some from among the membership sharing what God was doing in their ministries, and some from beyond the group including Anglican bishops, such as Tom Wright, formerly Bishop of Durham (quoted above), Paul Butler, the current Bishop of

---

39 Psalm 133:1
40 Psalm 133:2
41 Psalm 133:3a
42 Psalm 133:3b

Durham, and Mark Tanner, Bishop of Berwick. Although members of the committee differed in aspects of their theology, they all had a passion that people would come to know the Lord Jesus Christ. They also enjoyed each other's fellowship, including sharing light-hearted banter with each other as they met to plan the programme.

Ian enjoyed telling the story of the time he dared to invite David Holloway and Ken Gott to share at the same Mansion House meeting. He asked David, as an evangelical Anglican, to share about the importance of the Scriptures, and Ken, as a Pentecostal pastor, to share about the role of the Holy Spirit. To his surprise and encouragement, he found they slightly swapped roles with Ken focusing more on the importance of the Scriptures and David more on the role of the Holy Spirit in interpreting the Bible and guidance in general.

Robert Ward had been a close friend of Ian since he arrived in the city in 1980, and was a member of Ian's committee. Robert is a charismatic Anglican vicar who had been asked by the bishop to take over St Luke's Church in Spital Tongues, Newcastle that had previously closed. He believes that the fulfilment of Ian's vision of the coming together of different leaders from across the evangelical spectrum is a remarkable working of the Holy Spirit. He has expressed it as follows:

Before Ian called us all together, there was a high degree of criticism from the different camps for one another. The charismatics were considered "wacky"; they didn't really study the Bible, and were intemperate, while the conservative evangelicals were considered stiff, limited, dull and boring. All those ridiculous statements were made of one another, because we didn't know one another. The best way to get to know one another was over a meal. The Holy Spirit broke down the barriers, and we soon discovered that we loved and respected one another. We actually had a lot in common, including common problems in our lives and ministries. When the barriers are broken down, we are brought together in unity, and it is there that God commands the blessing. To my knowledge, and I get around a bit, it is unique in the country; I don't know of any other group intentionally started to bring together the charismatics and conservative non-charismatics. That is phenomenal.

Mike Johnson from the Newcastle Reformed Evangelical Church has also been a member of the committee from its inception, and is currently treasurer. He appreciated being asked by Ian to contribute to the work of the committee, and having fellowship alongside men such as Robert Ward with whom he would not otherwise have much contact.

Another member of the committee, George Curry, vicar of St Stephen's Church in Newcastle, is also from the reformed tradition. He very strongly understood that Ian wanted *"God's people to be outward looking and united, that their differences would be minimised, and what they share in common, new life, would be maximised"*.

Over seventy leaders continue to attend the meetings regularly, enjoying the meal, the fellowship with people with whom they would not normally meet, the talks about different ministries and the prayer for these ministries. Ian played a key role in the continuing success of the meeting from contacting people beforehand to remind them of it, to welcoming them to the gathering and ensuring that everything went smoothly. He was always keen to invite new people, encouraging them to come along, and following them up afterwards.

David Holloway, for example, spoke glowingly of the courteous, friendly way Ian and Helen greeted people, making them feel very welcome. He recognised the range of people there, from quite charismatic at one end to those much less sympathetic to charismatic worship at the other end. Although he would not call himself charismatic, David felt that he could still learn from those who would thus label themselves, believing that it was good to hear other views, even though he might disagree with them.

Tim Dunnett, senior pastor of Bethshan Church, now based in Washington, feels that only Ian could have brought the Mansion House gathering together because he has so many connections and he is held in such high regard across Tyneside churches. Tim has learned over many years in ministry that it is so valuable to talk to people who are of a different background from himself and with a different theological emphasis, and he believes that it was Ian who pushed him in that direction, with the Mansion House meetings playing a major role in developing this mindset of learning within a diverse group of leaders.

Sadly, in October 2017 Ian had to announce to the gathering that because of old age and ill health he felt that he was no longer able to lead the meeting. He had provided inspiring leadership bringing together such a diverse group of leaders. There was, however, a strong feeling that the forum was so valuable that it had to continue, and Paul Merton, formerly pastor of Westgate Road Baptist Church in Newcastle, took over its leadership.

Involvement in Different Activities

Although the Tyneside Leaders' Forum stands out as a major initiative established by Ian, there were other Christian groupings in which he was involved in the city and wider afield. Indeed, most of the committees that operated across the city, such as the Tyneside Evangelistic Council, the committee organising the Billy Graham relays from Sheffield to Newcastle in 1985 and Tyneside Youth for Christ, would have active input from Ian. He was seen as someone with a passion for the gospel and with a real love for those who needed to be saved. Eddie Stringer, one of the co-founders of Tyneside Youth for Christ, greatly valued Ian's input on the council of reference saying *"he always had a heart for young people"*. When he speaks, people know that he is giving words of wisdom with plenty of practical common sense.

He also wanted to see Christians built up in their faith and in their knowledge of the Lord. He was one of the co-founders of the Graduates' Fellowship in Newcastle and was a member of the Christian Medical Fellowship in Newcastle. One interesting group that he started was the local branch of the Evangelical Medical Fellowship of India. His involvement here started through Doctor Kuruvilla George (known as KG), a psychiatrist of Indian origin who worshipped for a time at Somervyl Chapel. It was partly through KG that Ian's son David took an interest in India and felt that God was calling him to work as a teacher out there, which he and his wife Gillian did from 1991 to 2005. KG went back to India and ran the Evangelical Medical Fellowship of India there, and Ian ran the Newcastle branch to provide prayer and practical support. In 1994, when Ian and Helen went out to visit David, Gillian and their family, KG invited them to speak at a three-day conference on Christian medical and family issues.

The importance of prayer is a passion that Ian has consistently held on to and is very central to his life. He continues to be involved in "Together in Christ", a prayer group of more charismatic Christians that meets in the city every Thursday. He also belongs to a more reformed group led by George Curry, vicar of St Stephen's Church in Elswick, praying for revival for the city and nation. Further afield, he has until very recently regularly attended conferences in Birmingham at the World Prayer Centre and has been greatly blessed by them.

Ian's involvement in the wider Christian ministries within the city and beyond has been an enormous blessing to those he has been working alongside. In the final two chapters we shall draw out the Christian leadership qualities that people respect so greatly in Ian, and try to identify the lessons we can learn from Ian's life and ministry that we can apply in our own situations.

Chapter Eight
Role-Model Leadership

Leadership Qualities

As we have seen, Ian had a tremendous influence on the lives of countless numbers of people with whom he worked or shared fellowship. A number of people in reviewing his ministry used the term "leadership presence" to describe a quality that Ian brought to wherever he was working, whether that was in the surgery, the chapel, the leadership forum or even the hospital cricket team during his training. It is, however, a bit of a nebulous term, and although we can recognise such a presence in great leaders, it may be helpful to identify the characteristics that help to provide that presence.

Tom Rath and Barry Conchie, two American consultants on leadership, have undertaken much research on leadership qualities. In one particular study they used a Gallup poll of over ten thousand people, who identified the qualities they most looked for in a leader whom they felt had influence on their lives.[43] The four most significant qualities from the survey were **trust, compassion, stability** and **hope**.

Trust is fundamental in establishing a relationship between those leading and those following. Sadly, trust is often missing in political circles and the corporate world, with people being sickened by broken promises and stories of scandals and fraud involving politicians and chief executives. It is particularly heart-breaking when a bond of trust is broken between a clergyman and his flock.

---

43 Tom Rath and Barry Conchie, *Strengths-Based Leadership* (Gallup Press, 2008).

The Bible, however, expects trustworthiness in leaders who have been appointed to serve God. In the Old Testament when Jethro, the father-in-law of Moses, was giving him advice about the need to delegate, he told him to *"select capable men from all the people – men who fear God, **trustworthy** men who hate dishonest gain – and appoint them as officials over thousands, hundreds, fifties and tens".*[44]

Similarly during the exile in Babylon, when plotting ministers tried to find fault with Daniel, *"they could find no corruption in him, because he was **trustworthy** and neither corrupt nor negligent".*[45]

Ian himself was seen as absolutely trustworthy in all aspects of his life. Over his long years of service on the Longbenton estate he was respected for his honesty, reliability and integrity. He could be depended on to do what he said and say what he meant. People knew that they could talk to him in confidence in the surgery, their own homes and in the chapel. Again in his wider ministry, church leaders absolutely respected his integrity. Indeed if Ian had not had the trust of so many people, the Tyneside Leaders' Forum would not have come into being and the Mansion House meetings would not have taken place.

It is natural that followers would expect their leaders to show **compassion**. From the Gallup survey, business leaders who are compassionate or caring are more likely to retain their employees, have more engaged customers and ultimately run a more productive, profitable organisation.

Jesus is the ultimate example of compassion. People followed Jesus, not simply because of the miracles he performed but because of the compassion he showed to the people he met. Matthew says that as he was journeying through towns and villages, teaching, preaching and healing, *"when he saw the crowds, he had **compassion**

---

44 Exodus 18:21
45 Daniel 6:4

on them, because they were harassed and helpless, like sheep without a shepherd".[46] Likewise, he had a deep care for individuals like the two blind men who, as they were sitting by the roadside, called out to him asking that they might receive their sight. Matthew says, *"Jesus had **compassion** on them and touched their eyes. Immediately they received their sight and followed him."*[47]

Ian and Helen were full of compassion for the people they were living alongside and working with. They both came from rather well-to-do backgrounds which were quite different from the backgrounds of most of the people living on the council estate of Longbenton, but, as Ken Prudhoe put it, *"Ian kept believing for great things and he continued to identify as much as possible with the local community, despite the obvious social differences, which mattered little to him."*

Simon Warren, whose family became Christians through the ministry of Somervyl Chapel, looking back recalled, *"How incredible it was that the son of a quite wealthy family, a graduate doctor, would come to Longbenton and live in the house next to a pub and invite us, the Warren family off the Longbenton estate, to make us his friends and love us and make us part of the family."*

As we have seen, Ian and Helen went out of their way to help the most vulnerable in the community, for example by visiting them or even providing hospitality to them. Sometimes it was through providing basic material needs. Helen recalls delivering logs and old wood to some of the ladies during the miners' strikes of that time, and Sue Glover, who worked as a receptionist in the surgery, recalls Helen nipping out from the surgery one day to get in supplies for a poorly lady. As well as leading the ladies' meeting, Helen would go out early each Monday evening to collect many of the older ladies

---

46 Matthew 9:36
47 Matthew 20:34

in her car and would always finish late after dropping them back at home after the meeting.

Compassion was at the heart of their ministry. In the same way that in the Old Testament Nehemiah wept in prayer over the state of Jerusalem,[48] Ian and Helen would weep in prayer over the people of Longbenton, praying for their needs, particularly for their spiritual needs that they might find Jesus.

In the Gallup survey, followers wanted their leaders to provide **stability**; in an ever-changing business and political environment, good leaders were expected to display stable core values that would help to provide their followers with a reasonable degree of security, even though they might be going through all sorts of turmoil.

Of course, the Lord God himself provides the ultimate stability and security. As the psalmist says:

God is our refuge and strength,
　　an ever-present help in trouble.
Therefore we will not fear, though the earth give way
　　and the mountains fall into the heart of the sea,
　　though its waters roar and foam
　　and the mountains quake with their surging.[49]

In the three decades or so that he was associated with Longbenton, Ian provided stability through his leadership in the practice and in the chapel. John McKale, who lived in Longbenton, spoke for many over the years by describing him as *"a great help just by being there for people and someone who was looked up to as a man of God"*. As we have seen over the years at Somervyl Chapel, there was much blessing but there was also division. Ian was there as a constant during times

---

48 Nehemiah 1:4
49 Psalm 46:1-3

of change. That does not mean that Ian stood still in his walk with God, but rather he learned from the people who were *"part of God's beautiful tapestry"*, as he described it, and he let God show him new things. He was there at the inauguration of Somervyl Chapel, he was there at its closing, and he remained stable and committed in the years between, a testament as to what God is able to do, using a man like Ian, working in a community such as Longbenton.

Hope was the fourth significant quality that followers looked for in their leaders in the Gallup survey. Here leaders were expected to provide direction and move the organisation to a better future. Employees were more likely to be engaged in their jobs if their leaders made them feel enthusiastic about the future, which of course can be very difficult at times of economic downturn or austerity.

When the Bible talks of hope, however, there is a vision of certainty, which is not dependent on the economic cycle. The psalmist sees his hope only in God: *"Guide me in your truth and teach me, for you are God my Saviour, and my **hope** is in you all day long".*[50] In his letter to the Romans Paul encourages his readers to look forward to the redemption of their bodies, *"for in this **hope** we were saved".*[51] When writing to Titus Paul says that we should live godly lives *"while we wait for the blessed **hope** – the appearing of the glory of our great God and Saviour, Jesus Christ".*[52] The writer to the Hebrews speaks of the certainty of God's promise, saying, *" We have this **hope** as an anchor for the soul, firm and secure."*[53]

Ian preached this message of hope. He could not promise the residents of Longbenton that they would always have secure jobs or that they would be free from pain in this life (although as a medical practitioner he would do his best to help them in this area), but he

---

50 Psalm 25:5
51 Romans 8:24
52 Titus 2:13
53 Hebrews 6:19

knew that they could have a better quality of life by putting their trust in Christ who would give them a hope for eternity. This was Ian's message of hope.

Ian also had another hope: a vision of what could be possible *"when God's people dwell together in unity"*.[54] This hope led him to start the Tyneside Leaders' Forum and the Mansion House meetings. As Ian looks back on his life he sees just how much God has answered his prayers. There is a unity among many church leaders across the North East, pastors and ministers relating, serving and seeking the good of their colleagues in other churches, a unity that did not exist fifty years ago.

Ian certainly had the qualities described above that were necessary to be an effective leader, along with other strong leadership capabilities such as having a clearly articulated vision, and being able to implement action and take risks to fulfil his vision. He had them in abundance, but that does not mean to say that he was equally skilled in all areas. Also by his own admission, he did not always get everything right. Deborah Ancona and her colleagues at the Massachusetts Institute of Technology published an article in 2007 entitled "In Praise of the Incomplete Leader", because they believed that leaders needed to work with others who would provide support where there were limitations in their own skillsets.[55] This is widely recognised. Very often the term "distributed leadership" is used to describe the sharing of leadership within an organisation, and of course many churches have, for some time now, established team ministries.

This was true for Ian as well. Within the practice, for example, it took a younger colleague, Valerie Wadge, to come in and modernise it and provide it with more strategic direction. Within the Christian

---

54 Psalm 133:1
55 Deborah Ancona, Thomas W. Malone, Wanda J. Orlikowski, and Peter M. Senge, "In Praise of the Incomplete Leader", *Harvard Business Review*, February 2007.

work on the estate, Ian was initially unsure about establishing a church building, and it took one of the ladies, Iris Bell, to keep prompting him in that direction until he himself realised that it was the right thing to do. In his leadership of the chapel, he relied very much on the work undertaken in the background by his close friend Lester Morgan who was church secretary over three decades.

Leadership: the Spiritual Dynamic

Ian was a natural leader in terms of the qualities he had and the capabilities he was able to display. For Ian, however, these qualities and capabilities were clearly God-given, to be used in his service. The apostle Peter wrote these words of instruction to elders in the early church that, of course, still apply today:

> *Be shepherds of God's flock that is under your care, watching over them – not because you must, but because you are willing, as God wants you to be; not pursuing dishonest gain, but eager to serve; not lording it over those entrusted to you, but being examples to the flock. And when the Chief Shepherd appears, you will receive the crown of glory that will never fade away.*[56]

These verses represent Ian's motivation in his work as a leader. He realised that he had a flock for which he was responsible and to which he was called to provide loving care. This meant trying to meet their needs, which he did as a doctor, but also trying to ensure that they went in the right direction without getting lost. The right direction involved finding and living for Jesus, the Chief Shepherd. It would be hard work, but being a shepherd was not meant to be a duty that had to be reluctantly undertaken, rather a work that he would

---

56 1 Peter 5:2-4

gladly do as God wanted. This responsibility was not to be taken for dishonest gain; on the contrary Ian was very generous with his time and money, giving hospitality to people in need and large sums of money to Christian causes at home and abroad. Nor did he lord it over the flock, expecting them to obey him because he was the leader, but rather he gave himself to the flock and, as such, was a wonderful example to them. Ian knew that his reward would come later when Jesus appeared and he would receive an imperishable glorious crown from his lord and master.

What was crucial to making Ian's leadership so effective was more than natural skills and qualities, but rather his intimacy with God. He had a deep love for God, with God's Holy Spirit controlling his life. He knew God was holy and to be revered, but he would also often refer to his heavenly Father as "Daddy God", with the same intimacy as Jesus would display in the Lord's Prayer, when he prayed, *"Our Father in heaven, hallowed be your name".*[57] Paul knew that this intimacy comes from the Holy Spirit who dwells within us as we become sons of God. In his letter to the Galatians, he writes, *"Because you are his sons, God sent the Spirit of his Son into our hearts, the Spirit who calls out, 'Abba, Father.'"*[58] The word "Abba" is an Aramaic word which demonstrates the intimacy of love for the Father. Ian knew this intimate love and it more than anything motivated his service for the Lord.

Prayer

It was through deep prayer that Ian developed this intimacy with God; he would come to him in praise and adoration and listen to what God was saying to him. It was in prayer that Ian, through the Spirit, would have a relationship with "Abba, Father". And it was in

57 Matthew 6:9
58 Galatians 4:6

prayer that Ian would seek the Lord for his own needs and the needs of others. These needs, however, were not only material needs or the need for good health and well-being, important as they were, but rather deep spiritual needs to know God in all his fullness.

Paul prayed for the Ephesians in a way that centuries later Ian would appreciate and put into practice:

> *For this reason I kneel before the Father, from whom every family in heaven and on earth derives its name. I pray that out of his glorious riches he may strengthen you with power through his Spirit in your inner being, so that Christ may dwell in your hearts through faith. And I pray that you, being rooted and established in love, may have power, together with all the Lord's holy people, to grasp how wide and long and high and deep is the love of Christ, and to know this love that surpasses knowledge – that you may be filled to the measure of all the fullness of God.*[59]

Paul is humbling himself before the Father because he is tremendously aware of what God has bestowed on his people through his grace. The *"for this reason"* refers to all the works of salvation and reconciliation achieved for us through Christ's death upon the cross which Paul had described in the previous chapter: *"For it is by grace you have been saved, through faith – and this is not from yourselves, it is the gift of God – not by works, so that no one can boast."*[60] Paul was so full of thanksgiving that *"he had to kneel before the Father"*. Ian was all too well aware that he was also a sinner saved by grace, welcomed into his heavenly Father's presence.

Like Paul, Ian wanted others to experience all that Christ had to offer his people. He wanted others to know Christ in a personal

---

59 Ephesians 3:14-19
60 Ephesians 2:8-9

way dwelling in their hearts through the power of the Spirit in their lives. He wanted their lives to be well grounded in the love of God and through this power in fellowship with the rest of God's people, to begin to know the amazing extent of God's love. Ultimately, he wanted others to *"be filled to the measure of all the fullness of God"*.

Prayer meetings were an integral part of the life of Somervyl Chapel and Ian would be there regularly participating or leading. There was a deep recognition that whatever he or others did would count for little unless God was active and at work and, for this reason, dependence on God and a ready and quick turning to prayer were of paramount importance. Ian was never hesitant to pray and to join others in prayer: prayer with and for the family at meal times, prayer with Helen in the evening, prayer when people came to visit or for fellowship.

He would pray for his patients to recover their health, and for members of the fellowship to overcome problems they might have, but what was more important to Ian was that he would pray that they would find Jesus and experience the glorious richness of his love.

As we have seen, Ian has a great prayer burden for the nation, and has encouraged others to join in prayer for our country. His attendance at the quarterly prayer meetings for revival is greatly appreciated by George Curry, the vicar of St Stephen's Parish Church in Newcastle, and who leads the meetings. George has put it as follows:

One of the passions that Ian and I share is that we would see the outpouring of God's Spirit in reviving power amongst his people so that they will be equipped to be the apologists in the world, to be the evangelists in the world, to do those good works that the Saviour has called us to do. That's what Ian and I share, and that's where I see him as a very dear brother. I would support my dear brother right up to the hilt in that and he would support me right up to the hilt. He will come to our quarterly prayer meetings for revival and he has this passion that the Lord would come down in a fresh way in power.

Learning from Ian's Leadership

Ian's spiritual influence on church leaders has been immense, and it continues to be so. Latterly Ian and Helen have been members of Bethshan, which now meets in a former working men's club in Washington, and their pastor is Tim Dunnett. Tim continues to receive from Ian inspiration and advice that he is able to apply in his own ministry. Ian would often pass a note to Tim at the end of the meeting saying what he had done well and what he might have done better. He would talk to Tim about what he believed was on the horizon and how Tim should incorporate these new developments in his ministry.

Ian's encouragement of Tim is but one example of how he has endeavoured to encourage, equip, resource and support other leaders over the decades. Whether it was by giving Dave Glover, in the early days of Somervyl Chapel, opportunities to develop his evangelistic skills that he would later use in the leadership of Killingworth Christian Fellowship, or by resourcing leaders across Tyneside through the Mansion House meetings, or by welcoming new leaders who came to the city or by giving people opportunities to grow, Ian wanted to see the region blessed as godly leaders developed their ministries in God's service.

Christian leaders need to ask God to provide them with the leadership qualities and capabilities that they need to carry out their mission for him, including putting them alongside others who can complement their skillset. Most important of all is developing a close relationship with their heavenly Father, seeking a passion in prayer that others may come to know Jesus.

This of course applies to all of us whether we are placed in positions of leadership or not. We all need to be *"rooted and established in love"* and to *"be filled to the measure of the fullness of God"*. We all need to find out, as Ian would put it, in which *"part of God's diverse and beautiful tapestry"* God wants us to serve him. We all need to have a passion for God's people and for those yet to know Jesus as their Saviour. As we do, we can look forward with Ian to God's revival in our land, seeing God changing people's lives and renewing our broken nation.

We shall then see God glorified and we can pray with Paul:

Now to him who is able to do immeasurably more than all we ask or imagine, according to his power that is at work within us, to him be glory in the church and in Christ Jesus throughout all generations, for ever and ever! Amen.[61]

---

61 Ephesians 3:20-21

Chapter Nine
Concluding Thoughts

As we look back on Ian's life, we can reflect on the way that God has been at work through, in and around him. Whether it was through Ian's own character and personality, his gifts, his passions, his training, or the different people God brought into his life and circle, or the medical and social culture of his day, or what he did not have as well as what he had, God used all of these as preparation in his life, as well as enabling Ian and Helen to be who they were and to achieve what they did.

Very often it is only as we look back and reflect on life that we see the threads that God weaves to make the rich tapestry. God wants to use situations that are difficult, and those that seem sad or strange, experiences we would not choose ourselves. He wants to enrich our lives and experiences and use them all for his glory.

God leads even before we begin to know him

Ian and Helen can both look back on their experiences of God leading them away from the career paths they were each following and into his calling. God responded to each at the point where they needed guidance and were expressing that in their individual ways. A prayer in the dark on a train, or a pin in the Bible, were both expressions of seeking God and looking to him.

God responded to each of them in a way that helped them move forward and not to look back. For Helen it was to confirm the desire that he had already put within her heart, while for Ian it was a bolt out of the blue and a call to something that he had never considered.

They had seen each other, talked, met and enjoyed companionship together. Lilian, Ian's aunt, had tried as a matchmaker, but it was only a number of years later when Jesus became part of both their lives that love blossomed and they really were ready to commit themselves to each other. Had Ian's Aunt Lilian seen something that they had not until later?

As we look back on their conversion, we see the hand of God through the concern of Helen's brother, the friendship of Ron Pont and the preaching of Archdeacon Harrison. God was clearly at work in and through people to bring them to a place of understanding the gospel, repentance and love for Jesus and commitment to him.

So in the ordinary and the extra-ordinary, we can see God at work in the lives of Ian and Helen even before they trusted him. Indeed, we know from Paul's teaching that *"he chose us in him before the creation of the world to be holy and blameless in his sight"*.[62] God establishes his purposes in our lives within eternity for his eternal glory.

God prepares us for the good works that he has prepared beforehand

God took the intelligent young man that Ian undoubtedly was, through his education at school and university and through his medical training, built on his natural leadership gifting and helped him to develop into a skilful, wise doctor who could lead at work and church. Helen went through different experiences, which developed her character and equipped her with medical and nursing skills, as well as those in secretarial work and administration. He led her to places and situations where she had opportunity to relate to a wide

---

62 Ephesians 1:4

range of different people, experiences she might have missed had she been successful in her application to study history at university rather than doing nursing. All of this was preparing them both for the roles they would have and the work they would do in Longbenton.

Fast forward to the experiences Ian would have as a doctor when he had the opportunity to relate to his Christian patients from a range of different churches, and see their love for God, albeit practising different ways of worshipping and serving him. This was great preparation for God's call to bring people of different denominations together across the region.

God has great purposes for each of our lives and, as Ian and Helen did, we too can take great strength from the fact that *"we are God's handiwork, created in Christ Jesus to do good works, which God prepared in advance for us to do"*.[63]

God leads through the people he brings around us

In his letters, Paul often refers to those who were his partners in the gospel. He refers to Timothy thus:

> *I have no one else like him, who will show genuine concern for your welfare. For everyone looks out for their own interests, not those of Jesus Christ. But you know that Timothy has proved himself, because as a son with his father he has served with me in the work of the gospel.*[64]

Where would Ian and Helen have been without the influence of others? God brought key people into their lives at just the right time: Ron Pont in Ian coming to Christ; Helen's brother Robin in her salvation; Ian Gunn-Russell in their calling to Longbenton; Lester

---

63 Ephesians 2:10
64 Philippians 2:20-22

and Margaret Morgan in supporting the vision for Longbenton; Iris Bell in inspiring Ian and Helen to consider building Somervyl Chapel; Doctor KG in encouraging Ian to start the UK branch of the Evangelical Medical Fellowship of India; Mervyn Spearing in his challenge to Ian to start the Mansion House meetings, and Sarah-Jane Biggart in her prophetic call to record this story.

Just as God used these and many others to influence Ian and Helen, so too has God used Ian and Helen to have similar influences on other people, some of whose stories are recorded in this book. Others' stories, we shall no doubt hear in heaven.

This is not only true for Ian and Helen, but also for each of us. God brings people across our paths, people he uses to bring encouragement, challenge, inspiration or direction. We would do well to pause and thank him for all those who have moved us forward in our walk with him and our lives for him.

God leads us though we do not have the theory

In the church today there is a right and good emphasis on learning and training, for example, on the techniques of evangelism, church planting or outreach. Sometimes, however, we can have all the theory and lack the courage and faith to act. Perhaps our emphasis is too much on how to get things right, as if our success is dependent on how well we do something, rather than on God's power.

The biblical view, however, is that we should be acting in faith, trusting in what God has said to us, even though we do not see what the completed tapestry will look like. The writer to the Hebrews in his eleventh chapter talks about the great Old Testament men and women of faith who followed God at his word, even though they could not see the fullness of his plan. He says about Abraham, for example, *"By faith Abraham, when called to go to a place he would later receive as his inheritance, obeyed and went, even though he did not know where he was going."*[65]

Ian and Helen had no mission or church-planting training, and yet God led them and those with them in Longbenton to form a "missional community". They began to function in that way well before the term was part of church and mission jargon.

They had courage, passion and faith that God would work, even if they did not have the words to express what they were doing. God took their prayer, passion for the gospel and their heart for the lost and the needy, and gave them the wisdom and people so that their lives and actions reflected God's heart for mission. They might not have been able to explain what they were doing or why, but God gave them the direction and the practical ways of living.

That does not mean that we should not seek to understand what we are doing. God, however, would encourage us, using Ian and Helen's lives as examples, to step out in faith without needing to know everything in advance.

God also uses what we do not have

This is true of the simple things like starting a practice with very few patients. Not having sufficient patients, and hence income, helped them focus on relating to the local community, on being present at the surgery and drawing people in. These were key factors in building up the contacts that were so helpful in the missional community that God was forming there.

Ian and Helen often looked up to Ron and Molly Pont, to John and Elsie Harris and to others who went abroad to serve the Lord in mission fields and mission hospitals around the world. This was something that they were not able to do because of Ian's poor

---

65 Hebrews 11:8

eyesight. God, however, used the fact that Ian did not have good eyes to take him to Longbenton. Poor and deteriorating eyesight was not something Ian wanted and he asked others to pray for him on many occasions, but still this did not disqualify him from serving God. God chose to use it to take him to Longbenton, the place God had prepared for him.

God also used the fact that Ian was not a minister in his own church to enable him to respond to preaching invitations in various churches and denominations across the region. Furthermore, as he was not running his own church, other ministers would be less concerned that he draw people from their congregations to join his own. Likewise, when Ian started the Mansion House meetings, it was very clear that it was not confined to leaders and churches from his denomination, because by that time he did not really have one. God used the fact that Ian did not really have a denomination or a label to broaden his reach and appeal to Christians across the spectrum.

Too often we can focus on our shortcomings or what we lack, and lose sight of the way that God uses even what we do not have as well as what we do.

God works in the culture and society of our time

Ian and Helen have seen huge changes in society during their lives. Cultural norms, working practices, family relationships and church structures have all changed beyond recognition. Medical practice is very different; there is much less of the family doctor and the small surgery in the locality. Estates built in the 1950s were communities with their own local butcher, independent greengrocer, milkman and doctor. They were hives of activity with children playing in the streets, mums pushing prams, and husbands stopping off for a pint at the working men's club as they returned from work at the end of the factory or shipyard shift. Now, Longbenton looks quite different during the day as it is more of a dormitory estate with people driving off the estate to work or to shop in the city centre, although local shops still provide essentials.

God called Ian and Helen to establish a work that would relate to the culture and society of the day and to reach the people of that place and generation. It was challenging, faith stretching, and demanding of time, energy and commitment, but it was relevant to the needs and culture of the community around them. The same approach may not seem possible in modern-day Longbenton, which is perhaps less of a community than it was in the heyday of Somervyl Chapel.

Yet the challenge on our modern estates is still there, and God can still use his church to relate to those who live there. It is heartening that so many new churches have been planted on our estates across the country allowing Christians to reach out to previously unchurched communities with the love of God. New ways are being developed to bring the freshness of the gospel to those who have been untouched by it. This is only a start and the surface only being scratched, but we need to pray that there will be a significant moving of God's Spirit across these estates.

In February 2019, the General Synod of the Church of England overwhelmingly agreed a motion to have a church established on every social housing estate in the country, thus reversing the previous trend of closing churches and withdrawing clergy from these estates. We need to pray that this motion will turn into reality and that, as Christians live and work amongst the residents of these communities, needs will be met, lives will be touched and people will turn to Jesus.

God has always been relevant to the culture and can always equip his people to relate to those around them, whatever the culture of the day. This is what Ian and Helen found as they responded to God as he led them in Longbenton. It will become the experience of many others who respond to the challenge of living and working for God in twenty-first-century urban communities.

Finally

It would not be right to put Ian and Helen on a pedestal and they certainly would not want us to do so. Reflecting on their lives, however, does teach us so much about God and his gracious leading, his relevance and his ability to take who we are and what we have, as well as what we do not have, to make a difference for his glory and his kingdom.

Each of us needs to reflect on our own story, on how God by his grace has acted in our lives, and as we go forward we *"may have power, together with all the Lord's holy people, to grasp how wide and long and high and deep is the love of Christ, and to know this love that surpasses knowledge – that you may be filled to the measure of all the fullness of God"*.[66]

May each of us know, as Ian and Helen know, that our life and experiences are indeed a thread in God's rich tapestry.

---

66 Ephesians 3:18-19